EPHESIANS:
THE LOVE WE LONG FOR

Scotty Smith

STUDY GUIDE WITH LEADER'S NOTES

New
Growth
Press

newgrowthpress.com

New Growth Press, Greensboro, NC 27404
newgrowthpress.com

Cover Design: Faceout Books, faceoutstudio.com
Interior Design and Typesetting: Gretchen Logterman
Exercises and Application Questions: Jack Klumpenhower

ISBN: 978-1-64507-061-0 (Print)
ISBN: 978-1-64507-062-7 (eBook)

Printed in The United States of America

27 26 25 24 23 22 21 20   1 2 3 4 5

CONTENTS

INTRODUCTION

Paul's letter to the Ephesians swings on a hinge. You can find the hinge about halfway through, near the end of chapter 3. Having explored the wonders of salvation in Christ, Paul kneels to pray that the Father would fill the Ephesians with that gospel. He asks that they "may have strength to comprehend with all the saints what is the breadth and length and height and depth, and to know the love of Christ that surpasses knowledge" (Ephesians 3:18–19). This is the boundless, timeless, endless, bottomless love we all long for.

From there, Paul swings open the door, as it were, and walks into the Ephesians' daily lives. The Ephesians were the fruit of Paul's missionary work, so he realized they were living in a culture that neither knew nor understood Jesus and his life-giving message. With this in mind, he addresses topics that range from patience and contentment and industriousness to parenting and singing and sex. But he never forgets how he got there. He keeps calling the Ephesians—and us—back to the hinge. The love we long for is the *why* and the *how*, and importantly the *who*, of a believer's whole life.

Like the other small-group resources in this series, this book follows that focus. Your goal will be bigger than merely to study Paul's letter to the Ephesians. You will also be practicing the discipline Paul himself followed throughout that letter: you will be returning again and again to the gospel of Jesus to see how it fills and powers your life as a believer.

HOW TO USE THIS STUDY

This guide will help you do this in a group study. Ephesians is written to the whole body of believers. Studying with other members of that body lets you benefit from what God is also teaching them, and it gives you encouragement as you apply what you learn.

Gospel-centered growth includes growing in awareness of your sin and in confidence that Jesus saves you in every way from that sin. Therefore, the group will be a place to share not only successes, but also sins and needs. Expect differences in how people participate. It's okay if some in the group are cheery while others are weary, if some "get it" quickly while others want to look more deeply, or if some are eager to share while others take it slowly. But because you'll be studying the Bible and praying together, also expect to "be filled with the Spirit" (Ephesians 5:18). Expect the Spirit to work and change people—starting with you!

Each participant should have one of these study guides in order to join in reading and be able to work through the exercises during that part of the study. The study leader should read through both the lesson and the leader's notes in the back of this book before each lesson begins. Otherwise, no preparation or homework is required from any participant.

There are twelve lessons in this study guide. Each lesson will take about an hour to complete, perhaps a bit more if your group is large, and will include these elements:

BIG IDEA. This is a summary of the main point of the lesson.

BIBLE CONVERSATION. You will read a passage from Ephesians and discuss it. As the heading suggests, the Bible conversation questions are intended to spark a conversation rather than generate correct answers. In most cases, the questions will have several possible good answers and a few best answers. The leader's notes at the back of this book provide some insights, but don't just turn there for the "right answer." At times you may want to see what the notes say, but always try to answer for yourself first by thinking about the Bible passage.

ARTICLE. This is the main teaching section of the lesson, written by the book's author.

DISCUSSION. The discussion questions following the article will help you apply the teaching to your life. Again, there will be several good ways to answer each question.

EXERCISE. The exercise is a section you will complete on your own during group time. You can write in the book if that helps you, or you can just think about your responses. You will then share some of what you learned with the group. If the group is large, it may help to split up to share the results of the exercise and to pray, so that everyone has a better opportunity to participate.

WRAP-UP AND PRAYER. Prayer is a critical part of the lesson because your spiritual growth will happen through God's work in you, not by your self-effort. You will be asking him to do that good work.

Ephesians will show you the unequaled dimensions of the love you have in Jesus. Whatever temptations you face and whatever accusations hound you, Jesus is greater. Hear his gospel anew, and be encouraged.

Lesson

THE SO-MUCH-MORE-NESS OF THE GOSPEL

BIG IDEA

There's nothing more than the gospel, just more of the gospel.

BIBLE CONVERSATION *15 minutes*

Before you begin reading Ephesians together, have each member of the group privately answer the question below using the first word or phrase that occurs to them. You'll share your responses later.

What does God give us if we have faith in Jesus?

There are many good ways to answer that question, and the apostle Paul mentions several of them at the start of his letter to the Ephesians. Ephesus was an important city on the eastern side of the Aegean Sea in modern-day Turkey. Paul had spent two highly successful years as a missionary there (see Acts 19:1–20). He wrote the letter years later, when he was a prisoner, addressing the church plant that had grown out of his work. But he does not begin by telling about his situation, or commenting on news he's heard about the Ephesians. Rather, he starts by celebrating what God has done and is doing.

Have someone read **Ephesians 1:1–14** aloud. Then discuss the following questions as a group:

Look through Paul's many answers to the question, *What does God give us if we have faith in Jesus?* Which of his answers are blessings you often think about, perhaps even matching your first-thought answer (which you may share now)? Which of his answers are blessings you seldom think about, and could be ways for you to enlarge your appreciation of the gospel?

In verse 3, Paul calls these "spiritual blessings." What are some ways they are bigger or better than the material blessings you've also received from God?

In verse 12 and again in verse 14, Paul says these blessings are to the praise of God's glory. It's easy to think of living for God's glory as a duty. What happens when you also see it as part of how you are blessed?

****

Now read the following article by this book's author. Have participants read it aloud, taking turns at the paragraph breaks.

ARTICLE

ASTONISHED BY THE GOSPEL

5 MINUTES

Like the Pevensie children stepping into Narnia, Prince Charming knocking on Cinderella's door, Jean Valjean colliding with the bishop's kindness—or my first day in Switzerland—some encounters leave us astonished, breathless, and wanting more. Such has been my experience with the book of Ephesians.

During my last semester at the University of North Carolina, I took a class in New Testament Greek. To my great surprise, although I had struggled with Spanish, I fell in love with Greek. It didn't hurt that I had a great teacher, no language labs, and the motivation of getting better equipped to understand God's Word.

Earning an A also got me an invitation from my professor to spend the following summer reading through Ephesians with him. God used that slow-paced, soaking-in-every-verse study of Paul's letter to throw the doors open on the Alps of God's love and the beauty of his Son. I've been back to Switzerland nine times since my first visit. In the same way, I also keep coming back to Ephesians.

Though I was already a Christian, "marinating" my way through Ephesians highlighted how much more there is of the gospel to understand and experience. I still believe this is true, fifty years into knowing Jesus. There's nothing more than the gospel, just more of it. This is clearly demonstrated in the first fourteen verses of Paul's letter.

After affirming his calling as an apostle of Jesus, Paul addresses us as saints who are "faithful in Christ Jesus." Sainthood isn't a measure of our spiritual maturity, but a revelation of God's great generosity. The word *saint* denotes one who is set apart, and we have been set apart by God for faith in Christ Jesus. The object of our faith matters most, not its size. We are faithful to the degree that we are full of faith in Christ Jesus. The gospel is a bold declaration of what God has done for us in Jesus.

This means God's "grace and peace" in verse 2 are received, not achieved. These two wonderful gifts are never reversed in the Bible. We will enjoy God's peace to the extent we experience his grace.

We sing the hymn "Amazing Grace," but what *is* truly amazing about grace? Verses 3 through 14 are one long sentence in the Greek—one magnificent run-on sentence of wonder. When I started studying this sentence in the summer of 1972, it felt like trying to stand up under the Niagara Falls of God's goodness and love. It was theology and doxology overload, and it still is.

In fact, I can't picture Paul sitting down at a desk to compose these introductory words to Ephesians. I imagine him pacing about the room, eyes wide open, arms extended heavenward as his stenographer strained to record everything that was flowing from his grace-flooded heart.

Joyfully trinitarian, Paul was a worshiper before he was a worker or writer. In this opening section of Ephesians, he adores the personhood of our God as he proclaims the propositions of our faith:

The Father is the origin of every good gift we receive. The Son is the basis and realm in which God blesses us. The Holy Spirit seals us, applies the gospel to our hearts, and guarantees our inheritance. God's grace claims our past, present, future, and forever.

The past blessing of election (vv. 3–6). Far from being confused, embarrassed, or chagrined about the notion of election, Paul celebrates the good news that we are chosen people, not choice people. From beginning to end, our salvation is entirely a work of God on our behalf. We didn't show potential; God showered mercy. Christians who understand God's electing grace should be the most humble and attractive believers in any community. For election is unto holiness and blamelessness before God (v. 6), not arrogance before men.

The present riches of redemption (vv. 5–8). Paul doesn't give us an exhaustive catalogue of the riches of grace. Rather, like the overture of a great symphony, he introduces main themes he will develop in the remainder of his letter. Notice how he begins with adoption, for there is no greater blessing than to be God's daughters and sons. Through Jesus's finished work and our union with him, every Christian enjoys the legal rights and personal delights of God's children. In the Beloved, we are loved—for Jesus is our substitute to trust before he is our model to follow. By Jesus's perfect life and sacrificial death, we are also redeemed (bought back by God, for God), forgiven (of all sins—past, present, and future), and lavishly enriched with grace.

The future hope of restoration (vv. 9–11). Indeed, every promise God has made finds its "Yes!" in Jesus, and God's promises are both personal and cosmic. The gospel isn't primarily about us going to heaven when we die, but about heaven coming to earth after death is destroyed. Our Father *will* bring to completion every good thing he has begun in us and in his creation. At the right time,

God sent Jesus as the sacrifice for our sins. In the fullness of time he will send him back to finish making all things new. Until then, sonship and heirship define us, and we are certain that God is at work in all things to accomplish his redemptive purposes in Jesus.

The forever blessing of worship (vv. 12–14). How are gospel-redeemed, grace-enriched, believers to live? As Paul states in verse 12, "to the praise of his glory"—a phrase he repeats twice in three verses. Every aspect of our lives is to declare God's glory, grace, and goodness. Like Paul, we too are to be worshipers before we are workers—now and forever. The rest of Ephesians will show us why and how to live this way.

DISCUSSION *15 minutes*

Think of all you've learned about God in your lifetime. What has been your high point? Tell why it's a truth you love and keep coming back to.

In your life, what does it look like for you to be a worshiper of God first, before being a worker for him? How might this affect *how* you work for God?

Lesson

EXERCISE

PAST, PRESENT, FUTURE, AND FOREVER

15 minutes

As you saw in the article, one way to keep a big view of the gospel is to think of it in terms of past, present, future, and forever blessings for those who believe in Jesus. (God's blessings are so full that those categories often overlap, but they are still a helpful framework.)

Begin this exercise by working on your own. For each category, read through the list of blessings Paul mentions. Rate yourself on how often you tend to remember and appreciate those blessings. If you can think of a specific way your behavior might change if you lived with more awareness of those blessings, note that also. Don't feel you need an answer for every blank, but answer where you can. After a few minutes, you'll have a chance to share some of your findings with the group.

PAST GOSPEL BLESSINGS

- God chose me before the foundation of the world.
- God planned for me to become holy.
- God chose me to be considered blameless in his sight.
- God created me with the purpose of becoming his adopted child.
- Jesus redeemed me at the cross (bought me back to belong to him).

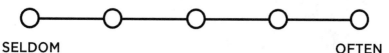

SELDOM   **OFTEN**

I believe and enjoy these blessings:

If I believed and enjoyed these past gospel blessings more often, I might _____.

PRESENT GOSPEL BLESSINGS

- All my sins are completely forgiven.
- I am an adopted child of God today, enjoying all those legal rights and personal delights.
- My Father lavishes grace on me, constantly helping me more than I deserve.
- By grace I am growing in wisdom, insight, and understanding of the mysteries of God's will.

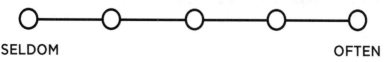

SELDOM   **OFTEN**

I believe and enjoy these blessings:

If I believed and enjoyed these present gospel blessings more often, I might _____.

FUTURE GOSPEL BLESSINGS

- I have an honored place in the future of heaven and earth, when God will make all things new and good again.
- God plans to complete his renewing work in me—this is my destiny.
- I will live with God to the praise of his glory.
- I will fully receive my inheritance as God's child.

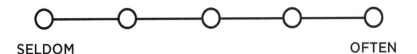

SELDOM   **OFTEN**

I believe and enjoy these blessings:

If I believed and enjoyed these future gospel blessings more often, I might _____.

FOREVER GOSPEL BLESSINGS

- My entire existence serves to glorify God, who works everything to fulfill his will for me.
- By giving me the Holy Spirit, my Father has kept all his promises to me and guarantees that he will continue to do so.
- Now and forever, I praise God who is most glorious.

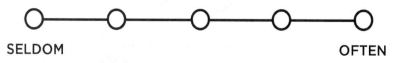

SELDOM   **OFTEN**

I believe and enjoy these blessings:

If I believed and enjoyed these forever gospel blessings more often, I might _____.

Once everyone has had a chance to answer for themselves, share some of your findings with the group. What do you find interesting? How would you like to grow?

WRAP-UP AND PRAYER *10 minutes*

If you want more joy in the gospel, a great way to start seeking that joy is to ask your Father to give it to you. Be sure to include such requests as part of your closing prayer time together.

Lesson

GETTING THE GOSPEL DEEP INTO OUR HEARTS

BIG IDEA

We grow as the Holy Spirit makes the truths of the gospel understandable to our minds and beautiful to our hearts, igniting love and devotion to Jesus.

BIBLE CONVERSATION *15 minutes*

After beginning his letter by celebrating the many blessings we have in Christ, Paul next tells the Ephesians how he prays for them. But this does not mean he stops telling about Jesus. Have someone read **Ephesians 1:15–23** aloud. Then discuss the following questions:

Look closely at Paul's prayer and identify what he asks God to do for the Ephesians. How do his requests compare with prayer requests you typically hear among believers? What's different, or similar, about his requests?

What do you like best about what Paul asks God to do for the Ephesians? Why do you like it?

15

By this point in the letter, it's clear Paul knows that the gospel is already powerfully at work among the Ephesians. Why would he pray for them to know even more about all they have in Jesus? Think of several possible reasons.

Do you talk this much about Jesus when you pray? Why might it be a good practice?

✳✳✳✳

Now take turns reading the article aloud, switching readers at each paragraph break. When you finish, discuss the questions that follow the article.

ARTICLE

"ADORACTION"

5 minutes

"It's alright, Scotty, I understand your youthful enthusiasm. But when you've been in New Testament studies as long as I have, you too will become quite bored with the whole enterprise."

I left my professor's office sad, yet determined. I was sad because this brilliant religion scholar was kind but so empty. It was the end of the semester and I had made an appointment to apologize for the bad attitude I showed through much of his class—a course titled Jesus in Myth, Tradition, and History. As a freshman in college and brand-new Christian, I was angry with my professor's assumption that the "Jesus story" was about 5 percent history, 65 percent tradition, and 30 percent myth. Though his one-sided presentation of the four Gospels upset me, nothing justified the smug body language I gave off in class.

My professor graciously accepted my apology, but I didn't accept his forecast. I knew Jesus was real, even though I was a neophyte in the Bible. I had a better *experience* of Jesus than a *theology* of Jesus. My religion class helped me realize I needed both, and I soon discovered that the gospel calls for both and delivers both.

My first model and mentor of "theology on fire" was none other than the apostle Paul himself. In this prayer in Ephesians, Paul shows us how the doctrines of the gospel lead to the delights of grace and how this moves us to greater devotion to Jesus. To know something biblically is never just academic, but also "adoractive"—adoration leading action. True faith will express itself in joy, worship of Jesus, and love for others.

In this passage, we see pastoring and discipling at its best. The first thing Paul does is to encourage the believers by calling attention to the clear evidence of the gospel at work in their midst. He commends their faith and love. Gospel faith is both *what* we believe and *who* we trust.

What the Ephesians were learning about Jesus, and experiencing in him, compelled them to have love for all the saints—Jewish and Gentile converts alike. Their faith expressed itself in love, and their love was a validation of the faith they professed.

Paul prayed as their spiritual father, wise to the intensity of spiritual warfare—which he will mention at the end of his letter. Satan knows he has lost Christians for eternity, but he will do anything he can to distort, divert, and destroy the work of the gospel in us and among us. He'll let us be religious or irreligious, moral or amoral, as long as we stay allergic to the grace of the gospel. But Paul knows that in spiritual warfare the best defense is a good offense. From the overflow of his own gospel astonishment and enjoyment of the Lord earlier in the chapter, Paul now prays the gospel deeper into the hearts of the Ephesian believers.

THE CONTENT OF PAUL'S PRAYER

Everything Paul asks of God is geared toward believers getting to know the Father and Jesus better and better. Jesus himself defined eternal life not in terms of quantity (living forever), but quality (knowing God). "And this is eternal life, that they know you the only true God, and Jesus Christ whom you have sent" (John 17:3). The gospel is the difference between just knowing about God and knowing *him* as he desires to be known. Paul prays for three specific things that are already ours in Christ. He prays that we would more fully understand and enjoy them. Paul prays that we might know . . .

1. The hope to which God has called us. *Calling* in the Bible has more in common with being subpoenaed than being invited. Through the gospel, God has subpoenaed us to hope. Let that sink in. With a view to the promised work of the Messiah, the prophet Zechariah actually referred to God's people as "prisoners of hope" (Zechariah 9:12). Because of the finished work of Jesus, God *will* complete the good work he has begun in each of his children and in his entire creation. Those most alive to this hope to which God has called us will live most joyfully in the mission God has given us. Hope, not fear, is the order of the day. Hope, not hype, is what the Spirit gives us. Hope, not denial, is the way of the gospel.

2. The riches of God's glorious inheritance in the saints. In the Greek, this sentence seems to have an intentional double meaning. God guarantees a glorious inheritance for all of his children that nothing can cancel, spoil, or rob. The life we will enjoy in the new heaven and new earth is beyond anything we could ever merit or imagine. But perhaps Paul is most zealous to underscore the other meaning of inheritance. Perhaps he wants us to understand that God has made us *his* inheritance. Our Father loves, treasures, and delights in us that much. Talk about doctrine becoming delight, and good theology becoming loud doxology!

3. The immeasurable greatness of God's power toward us who believe. The last thing Paul prays for is growth in our understanding and experience of how the Spirit is *for* us, *in* us, and works *through* us. He is *for us* because there are no contingencies with our God. He doesn't ask us for permission to do his work. That's great news for those of us coming from a legalistic, moralistic, or pragmatic background. The better we understand the gospel, the more we rest in the relief that God doesn't *try* to do things, as though failure is an option for our God. He isn't our co-pilot. God is the whole plane, sky, and destination. Secondly, Paul prays we will know how God's great power is at work *in us*. The Holy Spirit is a person at work, not a power pack we strap on. The Spirit witnesses to our sonship, telling us how much our Father loves us. He grows the fruit of Christlikeness in us. He comforts us in our journey between the resurrection and return of Jesus. And thirdly, God's power works *through us*; freeing us to relax and realize that none of us is the fourth member of the Trinity. He gifts us for ministry and does his best work through our brokenness and weakness. As we experience God's love in deeper ways, we are also freed to engage more directly in God's mission of restoration and redemption. As the Ephesians had already experienced in Paul's ministry to them, God's love flowing through us is one of the primary ways that the Father gathers others to himself.

DISCUSSION *10 minutes*

The author mentioned that we need both an experience of Jesus and a theology of Jesus. Which do you have more of? How might you get more of the other, and how would that be good for you?

How much do you think of eternal life in terms of quantity (living forever) instead of quality (knowing God)? How would you live differently in this life if knowing God and being with him was your greatest hope for the future?

Lesson

EXERCISE

2

PRAYING FOR AN "ADORACTIVE" LIFE

20 minutes

When we realize who Jesus is and that we pray as his people, we might think of all sorts of prayers we want to offer as we go through life with him. This exercise builds on Paul's praise of Jesus at the end of his prayer in today's passage. Paul gives the Ephesians (and us) a remedial course in Christology, showing us that good doctrine doesn't just lead to great delight, but especially to devotion.

As you look at each truth about Jesus that Paul mentions, think what you might want to pray because of it—perhaps something you've seldom thought of praying before! Like Paul's prayer, your prayer desires might be for an "adoractive" life where the truths you know about Jesus lead to adoration and devotion. Your prayer desires might include:

- Items of thanks and praise
- Requests that you (or someone else—especially those who don't yet know Jesus) would know or understand God better in some way

- Requests that you (or someone else) would live with greater hope or confidence in God in some way
- Requests that you (or someone else) would grow in devotion and service to Jesus in some way

Don't feel you have to think of a prayer for *every* truth about Jesus mentioned here. Just ponder the list and see which items spark a desire to pray. After you've had some time to think on your own, you'll be able to share some of your prayer desires with the group.

Jesus is my **resurrected Savior**, proof of God's immeasurable power toward us who believe (vv. 19–20).

Because of this, I might pray . . .

Jesus is my **ascended Advocate**, representing me from his seat at God's right hand in heaven (v. 20).

Because of this, I might pray . . .

Jesus is **Ruler of all things**, controlling all other authorities, powers, and people of great name (v. 21).

Because of this, I might pray . . .

Jesus is **King of the ages**, controlling everything about my future both in this life and the age to come (v. 21).

Because of this, I might pray . . .

Jesus is the **Victor over evil**, able to trample beneath his feet any evil that threatens me (v. 22).

Because of this, I might pray . . .

Jesus is the **Head of the church**, which he cares for as his body (vv. 22–23).

Because of this, I might pray . . .

Jesus is the **Filler of all things**, so that when I am filled by him I can be a blessing throughout his world (v. 23).

Because of this, I might pray . . .

When the group is ready, share some of your prayer desires with each other. Explain why you chose them. What hopes do you have for your prayer life?

WRAP-UP AND PRAYER *10 MINUTES*

Make sure your closing prayer time together includes several of the prayers you mentioned in the exercise. Encourage each other to follow up on the exercise and pray in the coming week as well, knowing that your Father in heaven is eager to listen to his children who are in Christ.

OWNING OUR NEED AND SAVORING GOD'S PROVISION

BIG IDEA

Our need for salvation is so great it took the life, death, and resurrection of Jesus to redeem us. Healthy Christians understand their ongoing need of the gospel and of the great help they have in the riches of God's grace.

BIBLE CONVERSATION *15 minutes*

Growing Christians are both brutally honest about their sin and delighted in their Savior. Chapter 2 of Ephesians demonstrates this. Paul picks up from his prayer for the believers in Ephesus by describing who they once were without Christ and who they have become in Christ. Have someone read **Ephesians 2:1–13** aloud. Then discuss the questions.

Paul gives humanity a most distressing diagnosis in the first three verses. He declares that without Christ we are spiritually dead, justifiably condemned under God's wrath, and enslaved in three ways:

1. We are *enslaved to the world*, consumed by what it offers.

2. We are *enslaved to the devil*, following the "prince" who sows rebellion and disobedience.

3. We are *enslaved to our own flesh*, living for the selfish passions and desires that come from inside of us.

When you think of who you are without Christ, which of these especially sounds like you, and why? How is it more than just a few occasional sins, but a slavery you couldn't escape from on your own?

Verses 4–10 are a famous passage about grace. Look through the passage and notice what blessings God's grace includes. Which is most meaningful to you, and why?

How do you feel about the fact that these blessings come by God's grace rather than because you earn them through good works? Is this mostly a point of doctrine for you, or a cause for joy? Explain.

DISMANTLED AND DELIGHTED

5 minutes

I love going to my dentist—an experience joyfully built into my schedule every six months. I go from the no-wait waiting room to a thirty-minute cleaning and a "looking good" from the hygienist, and I stroll out the door with new toothbrush and floss in hand. But not this time.

"Scotty, I think we need to go ahead and schedule you for a root canal." "ROOT CANAL!", I silently shouted to myself. Those are two words I hoped I'd never hear joined together and applied to a prognosis in my mouth. I used to chew sassafras roots as a kid, and I've fished many canals. But from as far back as I can remember, having a root canal was associated with passing a kidney stone, birthing a child, or giving bone marrow.

Dr. Hunter showed me my X-rays and explained how decay had infiltrated the root of one of my molars. Then he described the procedure he was recommending. At that point, I had a choice to make. I could dismiss his advice and live in dental denial: perhaps I could try to get better on my own or do a Google search for a less invasive way of dealing with a dying tooth. Or I could trust my dentist and submit to his plan. I chose wisely.

A month later, I'm glad to say, my experience proved my fears wrong. Though I would've preferred just another toothbrush and roll of floss, I am very thankful Dr. Hunter diagnosed my condition properly and prescribed the proper and necessary remedy.

That's what the gospel does. It reveals the depth of our need and the greatness of God's provision to meet our need. Whether it's our bodies, cars, or plumbing, we all want the right diagnosis. A misdiagnosis will always lead to even greater problems.

God robustly rebuked Israel's prophets because they "have healed the wound of my people lightly" (Jeremiah 6:14). We'd never just put a Band-Aid on leprosy or prescribe aspirins for E. coli. How much more care we should take when it comes to our need for salvation! Our need was so great it took the life, death, and resurrection of the Son of God to save people like us. To minimize our condition is to marginalize the gospel. It's a very good thing to own our need so we can savor God's grace.

This is why my spiritual father, Jack Miller, coined what is known as the double cheer-ups: "Cheer up! you are a lot worse off than you think you are. Cheer up! You are also more known, accepted, and loved than you ever hoped or imagined. *Both* are true because the gospel is true."

The gospel dismantles us before it delights us. It criticizes *us* before we cherish *it*. The sheer greatness of the gospel underscores our utter desperation for it. Notice how Paul establishes and celebrates the double cheer-ups in our passage from Ephesians.

THE GRAVITY OF OUR CONDITION (VV. 1–3)

Paul states that we were dead in our trespasses and sins. To trespass is to go beyond God's revealed will for our lives, and to sin is to fail to live up to it. It's important, however, to think of God's law not so much as a bunch of rules we keep or break, but as a design for relationship we violate. God made us to love, enjoy, and serve him with everything we are. Every expression of sin is rebellion against this life-giving relationship with God for which we have been created.

We were enslaved and stood justifiably condemned. By nature (and by choice, delight, and practice), we are "children of wrath, like the rest of mankind." We are children of wrath in two ways. Like selfish, stubborn children, we display anger, temper, and wrath when we don't get our way. But more importantly, we deserve God's wrath for all the ways we attempt to make our lives work with utter disregard for him.

How should we think about God's wrath? The wrath of God isn't the irrational rage, unhinged fury, or vengeance-filled ire of sinful humans. God's wrath is his appropriate response to everything that violates his beauty, goodness, and truth. God doesn't judge us in spite of his love, but because of it. His is a holy love. He cannot remain passive in the face of evil—the devil's or ours.

THE GREATNESS OF GOD'S PROVISION (VV. 4-7)

Some of the best words in the Bible only have three letters. *But* is one of them. It's a word of contrast. The gospel is the contrast between our need and God's response. Though we deserve God's holy wrath, he gives us his immense mercy. God is *rich* in mercy—not miserly, begrudging, or limited.

God loved us when we were dead in our trespasses, not when we demonstrated potential or were filled with remorse. We were dead—not metaphorically, but literally. The gospel isn't a redo, but a resurrection. It's not our second chance, but the second Adam (Jesus) doing for us what we could never do for ourselves. By his incomparable might, God made us alive, raised us up, and seated us with Jesus in the heavenly places. God didn't enable us to "turn over a new leaf." He made us a new tree.

Why did God expend such mercy and might on us? According to Paul, to show us the riches of his grace and kindness for us in Jesus. An incredible plan for our lives, indeed! Now and forever, God wants us to experience more and more of his grace and kindness. This affirmation absolutely blows the doors off everything I thought about God growing up. What about you?

THE IMMEASURABLE RICHES OF GOD'S GRACE (VV. 8–10)

God's grace is the basis, and faith is the means, by which God enriches us with the astonishing wealth of our salvation. Paul is adamant in affirming that even our faith is a gift from God. Faith isn't a muscle by which we merit God's favor. Faith is the empty hand which God fills with the riches of his grace.

We *are* saved by works, but not by our works. We are saved by the finished work of Jesus. Jesus's cry from the cross, "It is finished," wasn't hyperbole: Jesus accomplished everything we couldn't. We have no reason to boast in our own efforts or to bemoan their woeful inadequacy. All that is now replaced with resting in God's Son. God is the architect, financier, and builder of our entire salvation. "We are *his* workmanship."

We who used to walk in our trespasses and sins now walk in the works God has prepared for us. The gospel puts an end to all earning, but not to all effort. Works of guilt, fear, and pride are now replaced with labors of love. Hallelujah, we no longer work *for* God's favor, but *from* it.

DISCUSSION *10 MINUTES*

The author says the insight that "God wants us to experience more and more of his grace and kindness" blew up everything he thought about God growing up. What about you? What truths from this part of Ephesians produce a wonder in you that you never knew earlier in your life? Explain.

The article says, "Works of guilt, fear, and pride are now replaced with labors of love." Think about the works you do for God. Are you more tempted to work out of guilt, out of fear, or out of pride? What difference does it make when your work is a labor of love to God?

Lesson

EXERCISE

3

FAR OFF AND BROUGHT NEAR

20 minutes

The last part of our passage (vv. 11–13) tells how we were once far away from God but now have been brought near. In this exercise, you'll use those verses to remember and tell your own story about being brought near to God. Remembering helps you to be thankful and confident of God's continuing work in you. Telling others encourages them with stories of God's goodness. It also reminds us that every day we live and work next to people who may still be far from God and who are still waiting to hear about his grace and provision for our salvation through Christ.

NOTE: Not everyone has a clear conversion story. Some believers aren't sure when they first came to Christ, or may feel as if they've never known a time when they weren't a Christian. If that's you, use this exercise to tell more generally how God has brought you closer to himself or to tell about a meaningful step of growth in your life. Also remember that it's possible to have been a religious person who was still far from God (maybe Jesus was your model but not your Savior and source of righteousness). Likewise, if you aren't yet a believer or aren't sure, you can tell how God may be drawing you in or why you are interested in studying him. Adapt the exercise to fit your story.

Now work through the exercise on your own, writing down notes if that helps. You don't have to respond to every prompt, just those that help you tell your story. When the group is ready, you'll have a chance to share.

FAR AWAY FROM GOD

Before God saved us, we were CHRISTLESS—"separated from Christ."

How I was CHRISTLESS, not trusting in him:

We were HOMELESS—"alienated from the commonwealth of Israel."

How I was HOMELESS, without a Savior to rest in:

We were HOPELESS—"having no hope."

How I was HOPELESS, with no lasting peace:

We were GODLESS—"without God in the world."

How I was GODLESS, devoid of the one who created and cherishes me:

BROUGHT NEAR TO GOD

"But now in Christ Jesus you who once were far off have been brought near by the blood of Christ."

How God brought me to himself:

How I am nearer now than I used to be:

Now share some of your stories with the group. Tell what it means for you to have once been far off and to have been brought near to God.

WRAP-UP AND PRAYER *10 MINUTES*

As you leave, don't forget the gospel: "But now in Christ Jesus you who once were far off have been brought near by the blood of Christ." Marinate in every glorious word.

- *But now*—not in the distant future, but in this very moment.
- *In Christ Jesus*—the sphere and only basis of our salvation.
- *You who once were far off*—whether in a faraway country or living right next door to a church.
- *Have been brought*—you couldn't make the journey from death to life on your own, so God brought you.
- *Near*—how near? God has hidden your life in Jesus and adopted you into his family.
- *By the blood of Jesus*—the wrath God mercifully withheld from us, he poured out on Jesus fully.

There is no greater love than this. None. In your closing time together, include prayers of thanks for the stories God has worked and allowed you to share and hear. Ask him to continue his good work in you and to open your eyes to those around you who may still be longing to hear God's story of grace for the first time.

THE CHURCH ISN'T OPTIONAL

BIG IDEA

To be united to Christ is to become a member of God's every-nation family and Jesus's ever-growing church.

BIBLE CONVERSATION *15 minutes*

Where we left off in our last study, Paul had just reminded the mostly-Gentile believers in Ephesus that they had been far off from God but were brought near by the blood of Christ. Now he's going to show how this brings peace—both peace with God because Jesus has paid for the sins of all who believe (Jew and Gentile alike), and peace between believing Jews and Gentiles who are now all one in Christ. And he will show how this was all part of God's ancient plan to create something glorious.

Do you wonder what God was creating? Have one or more participants read **Ephesians 2:13–3:13** aloud. Then discuss the questions below:

Paul uses two illustrations from buildings to show how believers who might otherwise stay apart become one when they believe in Jesus.

1. Walls that used to divide us are torn down.
2. We are built together, like individual bricks making a grand building, into a people who become God's worship, witness, and dwelling place.

Which of these illustrations most makes you thankful to God or excited to be part of his people? Explain why.

In chapter 3, Paul explains how this joined-together, saved-in-Christ people ("the church" in verse 10) was God's unseen plan for the world all along. Why does it matter that we know this? What are some ways it might change our attitude or approach to being together?

Imagine some of the believers in Ephesus wanted to be Christians "on their own," apart from the rest of the church. Based on this passage, what would be some of Paul's objections?

****

Now take turns reading the article aloud, switching readers at the paragraph breaks. Discuss the questions when you finish.

"JUST GIVE ME JESUS"

I de-churched long before it became a popular trend for Christians in our day. That's not a boast, just a part of my late-1960s story. With near mantra-like passion, I can still hear my new-in-Christ self saying, "Don't give me theology or church, just give me Jesus." I was proud then, but gladly eat gospel crow now.

Like most of the things we learn to regret, there's a backstory. I grew up in a small community and Presbyterian church that were neither liberal nor conservative, just Southern. Religion was a part of our cultural psyche and weekly cycle. The gospel was assumed, because everybody I knew was a Christian by virtue of being born, not born again. All you had to do to go to heaven was die. A prayer before meals was more habit than gratitude, and though I'd never put anything on top of the Bible in my headboard, I never opened its pages.

There's never been a day in my life when I haven't self-identified as a Christian. Until the day I became one. I put my faith in Jesus as a senior in high school, when a friend persuaded me to go with him to a local movie theater to see a Billy Graham movie, *The Restless Ones*. I consciously believed the gospel for the first time. My relief, peace, and joy were palpable. But it didn't take long for anger, resentment, and cynicism to be just as real.

Why hadn't my church told me about a personal relationship with Jesus? I felt deceived and robbed, sad and mad. It was 1968 and a cultural revolution was underway. The Vietnam War and the Beatles invasion assailed my monochromatic way of life. Spiritually, the Jesus Movement made its way to North Carolina. The wind of the Spirit was fanning the flames of celebration and protest. I joined both.

Looking back, I love my passion but grieve my naiveté. To me, the word *theology* was synonymous with dead doctrines, and *church* represented lifeless religion. I replaced the phrase *the church* with *my church*, as I assumed the right to define what a real church is. Here's to the mercy and patience of Jesus.

It felt right and good to declare, "Don't give me theology, just give me Jesus." It felt good, but it was egregious. For every time we speak the name Jesus, we are doing theology. Which Jesus are we talking about? Jesus, the moral model to follow for earning one's way into heaven? The Jesus of American racism—very white and disparaging of black people? The Jesus of the prosperity gospel—who exists to make me happy, ridiculously wealthy, and cancer-free? The Jesus of post-modernity—a conflicted social misfit who may or may not have even existed? The Jesus of every major cult—not God incarnate, but man becoming godlike? Because Jesus matters, theology matters.

And what about the other half of my misinformed couplet: "Don't give me church, just give me Jesus." I now realize how much that would be like me saying to my wife, "Don't give me the complexities of marriage and intimacy. Just give me sex." Or to my employer, "Don't give me responsibilities, expectations, or a review. Just pay me." Or to my friends, "Don't expect me to enter your story, passions, and struggles. Just make me feel awesome about me." Ludicrous? Worse, idolatrous. Whenever I define anything or anyone primarily in terms of benefit to me, I am committing idolatry.

Because Jesus is who he claimed to be, the church is what he declares her to be: his body in the world, a beloved mess, his treasured bride, the means by which he is showing the gospel to the entire cosmos. Look at Revelation 2 and 3, and you'll see that no one has greater affection for the church, or offers more criticism of her, than Jesus. Let's look at how Paul establishes the necessity and preciousness of the church.

JESUS OUR PEACE (2:14-22)

Paul joyfully proclaims that Jesus himself is our peace—*our*, in deliberate contrast to *my*. Knowing Jesus is personal, but it's not individualistic. Sin has made a mess of everything, both our relationship with God and the way we relate to one another. Paul wants the recipients of his letter, both Gentiles and Jews, to understand that the gospel is the way God reconciles sinful individuals to himself and also how he reconciles us to each other.

God's eternal purpose was to make what verse 16 calls "one new man"—a new humanity not merely marked by the absence of conflict but by the presence of reconciling love. God's love for us puts an end to every form of racism, tribalism, and nationalism.

Prophets envisioned this day, and Jesus's apostles announced the arrival of the day in Acts 2. Together, the prophets and apostles are the foundation of this living-temple family, with Jesus as the cornerstone. Let this sink in. The new temple God is erecting isn't made from Jerusalem limestone, but resurrected lives. It isn't rocks lifted from a quarry, but lives redeemed by God's grace.

HIDDEN THINGS REVEALED (3:1-6)

Paul makes it unmistakably clear: the reconciliation and integration of God's people into one family wasn't a novel idea or Plan B. As the history of redemption unfolds from Genesis through

Revelation, generation to generation, nation to nation, city to city, and heart to heart, it has always been God's plan to have one big, united, diverse family to delight in forever—a people to fill with his presence, his Spirit, and his praise.

Paul refers to his insight into God's plan for the nations as a mystery, not because it's a strange teaching but because it was previously hidden. On this side of the finished work of Jesus, old covenant shadows are fulfilled with new covenant substance. God's promises pregnant with grace are giving birth to a multitude of daughters and sons from all nations and tribes—a number so great that Revelation 7:9 says no one can tabulate it. The whole family of God are heirs of eternal hope, members of Jesus's body, and partakers of God's promise. What a grand and glorious story! This is how big Paul's gospel was. How about ours?

THE SHOW AND TELL OF JESUS'S CHURCH (3:7–13)

Saving the best for the last, in verse 10 Paul now refers to this gospel-created grace-family as "the church." What and who is the church? The church is a beloved family, created by God and redeemed by the gospel, called to be the primary means by which God shows and tells his story of redemption in Jesus. But who is God's intended audience for "bringing to light" his "eternal purpose" and "manifold wisdom"? It is not just our neighbors and the nations, but "rulers and authorities in the heavenly places" (v. 10).

As meager and meaningless as she may seem to the naked eye, the church's place in the heart and economy of God is magnificent. Through the church, God puts the cosmos and all powers on notice: Jesus Christ is Lord, the Savior of the world, the One who is making all things new. Through Jesus, and only through Jesus, Jew and Gentile both have bold access to a throne of grace. This is the church's meaning, message, and mission.

Do you criticize, bemoan, and grieve what the church often looks and smells like? Jesus beat you to it. Should you dismiss her? Based on this one portion of Scripture alone, it's not a good idea.

DISCUSSION

Even if you've never been tempted to say it aloud, recall a time in your life when you may have started to think, "Don't give me theology or church, just give me Jesus." What made you think that way? How were you, like the author, also being shortsighted?

In what ways is a church service a foretaste of the life we will enjoy when Jesus returns? If you went to church thinking of it that way, how might it change your attitude or actions there?

Lesson

EXERCISE

CHURCH IS . . .

Each of us has several ways we think about church. In this exercise, you will first note some of the ways you might tend to think of church and then some ways Paul thought of church. Work through the exercise on your own first, and then share some of your findings with the group.

PART 1: HOW YOU THINK OF CHURCH

Note some of the responses below that most closely fit how you tend to think. (Some of the responses are good ways to think about the church that are true of it—though maybe not the *best* way to think.)

To me, church is . . .

☐ **A resource (one of many).** "I find a good church to be useful. It gives me things like teaching that I and my family need."

☐ **A habit.** "I've always gone. It's probably good for me. People ought to go to church, you know."

☐ **A spiritual pick-me-up.** "A church with the right music and preaching really does my soul good!"

☐ **A social outlet.** "My friends are all there. It's how I build community and stay connected."

☐ **A spiritual duty.** "God expects me to be in church. If I don't show up, that's negative points for me."

☐ **A way to impress.** "I want the pastor or others to see that I'm there—and serving, too. I'm a good servant at church. Have you noticed?"

☐ **A relic.** "Church is an outdated idea. It's good for when I'm sentimental, but mostly I'm over it."

☐ **A difficult slog.** "It's never really right for me, not quite what I want or need."

☐ **A hurt.** "There are things in my past that make church painful."

☐ Other: _____.

PART 2: HOW PAUL THOUGHT OF CHURCH

Now note some of Paul's thoughts on church that you feel might be most helpful or encouraging to you if you were to approach church with them in mind.

To Paul, church is . . .

☐ **The end to divisions.** "I can come together, in the peace of Jesus, with people who are otherwise different from me."

☐ **The purpose of redemption.** "It's a foretaste of heaven for me—the assembly of Christ's saved people."

☐ **The hidden mystery revealed.** "God's people waited thousands of years for the praise and salvation of the nations. Now I'm part of it!"

❏ **Access to God.** "What could be better than to join God's people as we come before him with boldness?"

❏ **The witness in heavenly places.** "Angels are watching. Heaven erupts in praise when I join God's people to worship the One who has saved us."

❏ **The breakdown of hostility.** "Yes, church isn't always how I'd like it. That's part of the point. I'm giving up my own demands. It's glorious."

❏ **The temple that lasts.** "The church is timeless. Many other things I do won't last, but my fellow 'bricks' and our worship will extend into eternity."

❏ **The place where God dwells.** "God is with his people. Nothing is better for me than to be there too!"

❏ Other: _____.

Share some of what you noted with the group. How would you like God to change your approach to church? What might make change difficult? How might your daily actions or your worship change if your approach to church changed?

WRAP-UP AND PRAYER

This might be a good day not only to pray that God would change you, but also to pray for your church.

5

GROWING IN THE KNOWLEDGE AND LOVE OF JESUS

BIG IDEA

There is only one love that is better than life, only one love that is enough to meet our needs and satisfy our longings, only one love that will never let go of us: God's love for us in Jesus. The Christian life is a now-and-forever journey of growth in the much-more-ness of this love.

BIBLE CONVERSATION   *15 minutes*

It would be one thing if Paul wrote Ephesians from a veranda overlooking the Mediterranean Sea with refreshing libation in hand and servants fanning him with palm branches. But he was actually a prisoner. That's important to remember as we look at his second prayer in this letter. In the midst of a very difficult situation, Paul enjoyed rich, robust intimacy with Jesus—the very reality he prayed for the Ephesian believers. Paul never asked the Ephesian church to pray that God would get him out of prison. Rather, he prayed that God would get more of the gospel into the church. Paul wasn't looking for their pity, he was working for their joy.

Have someone read **Ephesians 3:14–21** aloud. Then discuss the questions as a group.

If you were to borrow one phrase from Paul's prayer to use in your own prayers, which would it be, and why?

Notice how Paul mentions strength and power in verse 16. Based on the rest of his prayer, what do you think Paul would say are some keys to a powerful Christian life? If God has worked this kind of power in your own life, tell about that.

Based on verses 20 and 21, how certain can we be that God will answer Paul's prayer? What can we say about *how* God will answer it? How often do you think this way about your prayers? Explain.

****

Now take turns reading the article "Kneeling Before the Father" aloud, switching readers at the paragraph breaks.

KNEELING BEFORE THE FATHER

5 minutes

How we address God, what we pray for, and how much time we spend in his presence are quite revealing in a most helpful way. Before I became a Christian I actually prayed quite often. It was more out of fear than faith, and more routine than real, but I did pray. I mastered "Now I lay me down to sleep" by age three, and we always "said the blessing" before meals—except when eating in public, which might have been a little pretentious or embarrassing.

The first prayer I remember learning at our church was the one we commonly label the Lord's Prayer. It was a weekly part of our worship service, along with singing the doxology and reciting the Apostles' Creed. I learned the Lord's Prayer by mimicking what I heard.

"Our Father, who art in heaven, hallowed be thy name . . ." As I write out those opening words, I see myself parked next to my mother, dressed in my Sunday school clothes—sitting as still as possible to avoid being shushed for squirming. My mom didn't want her boys distracting fellow worshipers.

What I remember most about saying the Lord's Prayer as a young child was that confusing word *hallowed*. What did *hallowed* mean? The closest word I could associate *hallow* with was *hollow*. "Hollow be your name . . ." Indeed, God's name, like my spiritual life, was quite hollow to me at that point. You may have a similar story.

But, as we're learning in Ephesians, God delights to fill our hollow hearts with his free grace. He takes us into the shallow end of the gospel pool in preparation for swimming in the deep ocean of his love. Paul makes this process beautifully clear in this section of his letter. Here we meet the praying, delighting, worshiping, petitioning Paul—wooing us further up and further in to the riches of the gospel.

I cannot overemphasize how much God has used this particular portion of Ephesians in my life, and continues to do so. As I first meditated my way through this prayer, I found myself just as captivated with Paul's heart as with his theology. The two, obviously, go hand-in-hand.

PAUL'S PRAYER

Paul bowed his knees before the Father as he prayed. To kneel in prayer was a sign of deep emotion and sincerity, for the usual prayer posture for a Jew was standing. Paul's intense feelings were an indication of his love for the Ephesian believers and, even more, a sign of his adoration of the God of all grace. Paul addresses God as Father, but not just as any father. He is "the father from whom all fatherhood derives its meaning"—a translation I settled on while working through the text with my Greek professor. This means the very concept of *father* comes from God to us.

Psychiatrist Sigmund Freud suggested the idea of *father* starts with us, and we project it onto an imaginary "god" of our own making.

He was right about our longing for a perfect father, but totally wrong about where this craving comes from. The God who made us built into our DNA a most holy, insatiable longing to know him as our Father. No early father can possibly be to his children what our heavenly Father alone can be.

So what, exactly, did Paul ask the Father to give every believer (including you and me) and all churches (including ours)? In the midst of Paul's doxological outburst, I see three primary petitions.

1. Know Jesus more intimately. This is what Paul means by "Christ dwelling in your hearts through faith." Once we become believers, Jesus comes to reside in us—in our "inner being." Though there aren't degrees of receiving Christ, there are degrees of knowing him. This is why Paul prayed in Philippians 3:10, "I want to know Christ." He who knew Jesus much better than you and I do wanted to know him even more. The Spirit is pleased to create the same desire in us.

2. Experience more of Jesus's love. We who have already been "rooted [agricultural metaphor] and grounded [architectural metaphor] in love," are to continue to grow and give evidence of the incomparable love of Jesus. We will never exhaustively know Jesus's love. Like the gospel, so with the love of Jesus—there's always more. We can, however, grow in our knowledge of Jesus's love "with all the saints." Paul stresses our shared life and inter-dependence as the body of Christ. It is precisely in the messiness of life in the body of Christ that we have great opportunity to discover more of the multi-dimensional love of Jesus.

3. Become more like Jesus. Paul prayed with a view to the day we will become "filled with all the fullness of God." This is a prayer for our Christlikeness. The goal of our salvation is not getting us into heaven, but heaven getting into us. We live between the most wonderful bookends of our justification in Christ and our glorification by Christ. This in-between journey is called sanctification—a process that is often quite painful. But with the certainty of Jesus being our righteousness (justification) and the assurance we will be made like him one day (glorification), sanctification becomes a process of quicker, deeper, and more joyful repentances.

CAN WE BE CERTAIN GOD WILL ANSWER PAUL'S PRAYER?

With a huge crescendo of praise, Paul grounds the fulfillment of his petitions in the work of the entire Trinity. My hunch is Paul finished this prayer still on his knees, but with his hands lifted skyward in adoration.

"Now to him who is able to do far more abundantly than all that we ask or think." He who gave Jesus for us will certainly give everything else we need to complete our salvation. How much will our Father do on our behalf? If you're like me, you can ask and imagine a *whole* lot. But according to Paul, we still underestimate God's generosity and faithfulness.

What is the measure of God's ability? It's "according to the power at work in us"—that is, according to the peerless might of the Holy Spirit, who raised Jesus from the dead. This is the power that is at work in us—not *by* us, but *in* us.

The Holy Spirit isn't a power we use to make ourselves like Jesus. We don't strap him on like an energy pack. The Holy Spirit inhabits us like a complete restoration crew. He is the third member of the Trinity, alone able to transform, heal, and free us. God gets all the credit for our desire and doing. The pressure is off. This doesn't mean we are passive in the Christian life. But it does mean we are entirely dependent, and God is entirely dependable.

What is the ultimate goal of Paul's prayer? "To him be glory in the church and in Christ Jesus throughout all generations, forever and ever. Amen." Paul envisioned the day when the church will be absolutely filled with the glory of God—the day when Jesus returns "to be glorified in his saints, and to be marveled at among all who have believed" (2 Thessalonians 1:10).

DISCUSSION *10 MINUTES*

Many different emotions can be appropriate for prayer—just look at the variety in the Psalms! What does *your* emotional life tend to look like when you pray? How does your posture, or the way you address God, reflect what's going on inside of you? Explain.

The article says our Christian growth should be "a process of quicker, deeper, and more joyful repentances." How do you react to that idea? What do you find appealing about making that the goal for your life, and why?

Lesson

EXERCISE

5

DIMENSIONS OF LOVE

20 minutes

Paul prayed that, in fellowship with other believers, we would grow in our experience of the multi-dimensional love of Jesus. What are we to make of his language that mentions *breadth, length, height,* and *depth*? We can't say for sure what was in Paul's mind, but we do know for sure some of the love that is in Jesus's heart.

For this exercise, work on your own to fill in what Paul may have been thinking in his prayer, using what you know about Jesus from your study of Ephesians so far or from elsewhere in the Bible. Try to mention things that are especially meaningful to you or give you wonder. This time, fill in every blank, since forcing yourself to come up with responses will help you think deeply about the love of Jesus. After everyone finishes, you will all share your responses. Together, your group will produce a multi-dimensional look at Jesus's love formed by "all the saints"—all of you!

God's love is SO BROAD it includes both _____
and _____.

God's love is SO LONG it starts with _____
and extends all the way to _____.

God's love is SO HIGH he gives me both _____
and _____.

God's love is SO DEEP that, as hard as I may try, I cannot see the
end of his _____ and his
_____ for me.

Now share your responses with the group. Which of your responses
are particularly meaningful to you, and why? Which responses
from others help you see Jesus's love a little better, and how?

WRAP-UP AND PRAYER *10 MINUTES*

It's easy to see why Paul referred to Jesus's love as a love that "surpasses knowledge." Even by pooling your knowledge, your group
has only seen some of it. As you end your time together with
prayer, you might use Paul's prayer as a template for some of what
you ask your Father to lovingly give you.

Lesson

CULTIVATING A CULTURE OF GRACE

BIG IDEA

The gospel calls Christians to build a culture of grace wherever we worship, live, work, and play.

BIBLE CONVERSATION *15 minutes*

Every company, club, team, or group emanates a culture—an ethos created by design, or else by default. The same happens in churches. When God's grace is cherished among his people, it creates a very unique culture. In the first three chapters of Ephesians, Paul gave us a grand introduction to the theology of the gospel of grace. Now, as we move into the second half of his letter, he will give us practical implications of this gospel. He begins by showing how God's grace reshapes the culture believers share.

Have someone read **Ephesians 4:1–16** aloud. Then discuss the questions.

In verse 2, Paul describes a life worthy of our calling as one of humility, gentleness, patience, and loving forbearance. Why are these attitudes sometimes hard to maintain within the church, of all places? Why do you personally need Paul's reminder?

What is Jesus's purpose for gifting some believers to be the church leaders mentioned in verse 11? How is this purpose different from other purposes of leadership you have encountered outside the church? Why would leading Jesus's church be a different kind of leadership?

How would you summarize the difference between a believer who is like a child (v. 14) and one who is growing up (v. 15)?

****

Now read the following article aloud, taking turns by paragraph.

ARTICLE

A TRULY CHRISTIAN CULTURE

5 minutes

Dear Scotty,

Though I spent four weeks visiting your church, we never met. That's on me, not you. I came to Franklin to help my daughter, Sally, (name change) with her first child—my first granddaughter. Because she was nursing, I had to go to church with her so Sally could enjoy the service. I sat on the very back row, holding the baby. That's the only way my daughter could have gotten me into any church.

I hate church, distrust preachers, and am annoyed by most Christians. The church people I know back in Florida aren't any different from people who sleep in on Sunday mornings. They're just as selfish, greedy, and prickly. But here's the thing: sitting in the back of your church for four Sundays was different. I felt welcomed and respected, and I noticed all kinds of people there—rich and poor, well-dressed and shoeless.

It was the first time I've been in a sinner-safe church. It didn't feel like a religious show. People seemed real and humble. Everyone seemed to need what you were talking about, including you.

Most of the preachers I've heard seem angry, arrogant, and a bit emotionally constipated. I didn't get that vibe in your church. My daughter said it was God's grace I was seeing. Perhaps. I wish I there was a church like yours in South Florida. Maybe I'd risk a visit.

Anyway, thank you, Karen Anderson (name changed)

∗∗∗∗

Of all the letters I've received in forty years as a pastor, none has meant more to me than this one. Karen was describing a unique culture—an ethos of grace that permeated Christ Community Church, in Franklin, Tennessee. The gospel of God's grace took hold among a diverse group of people coming from legalistic, non-believing, and religiously burned-out backgrounds. God sovereignly decided to drop a gospel bomb on downtown Franklin, and we had the joy of being the collateral damage. A culture of grace emerged from the rubble. Let's look at some features of this gospel culture as described by Paul.

A CULTURE OF WORSHIP AND WELCOME (VV. 1–6)

A culture of grace can only be cultivated in vital, intimate relationship with the God of all grace—Father, Son, and Holy Spirit. That's because this culture is supernatural, not superficial. It springs from the life of God in our hearts and in our midst. God's welcome fuels our worship and compels us to offer his welcome to others.

Notice how Paul intentionally lists each member of the Godhead. There is one Spirit, one Lord (Jesus), and one Father—one God in three persons, each intently involved in our salvation. Together, they are the fountain of grace because they are the source of all grace. Throughout eternity, the members of the Trinity have enjoyed the fullness of joy and intimacy they long to share with us.

This triune God calls us as one body to one hope, through one faith, by one baptism. All these *ones* underscore the unity, not uniformity, we share as the family of God. We come from many different backgrounds, worldviews, and stories of brokenness. Only God is able to create unity from such diversity and complexity.

Paul calls this "the unity of the Spirit," not merely a united spirit. The common life we share is no mere *esprit de corps*, but a sharing in the life of God—who is "over all and through all and in all." It's a oneness the Holy Spirit creates by uniting us to Christ and then to one another. It's a unity we are to treasure and guard because of our calling to reveal what God is like to the world.

In a culture of grace, a commitment to this unity trumps individualism and condemns divisiveness. Each of us matters, but none of us is the point. As Paul writes in Philippians 2:3, we "count others more significant" than ourselves because we esteem Jesus above everything! Why do we value Jesus so highly? The next metaphor Paul uses explains that part of a culture of grace.

A CULTURE OF HUMILITY AND GRATITUDE (VV. 7–10)

I grew up loving parades, from our local, small-town Christmas parade all the way to Macy's annual Thanksgiving extravaganza. But Paul describes a different kind of parade. The work of Jesus is presented in terms of a Roman warrior parading though his city after conquering a rival, with captured prisoners and seized treasures following behind in a parade of shame.

The gospel turns this image upside down. Instead of a parade of shame, we are captives in a parade of grace. Jesus is regaled as the victorious warrior who didn't just triumph *for* us, but *over* us. A proper understanding of the gospel won't lead us to say, "At the end of the Bible, we win." Rather, "At the end of the Bible, the Lamb triumphs over all things, including *us!*" Jesus isn't the captain of our rugby team; we're a part of the mess he came to redeem.

Lesson 6: Cultivating a Culture of Grace 59

After his descent (which refers to his incarnation and death), Jesus was raised and he ascended to the right hand of our Father. One day, God will fill the cosmos with the glory of Jesus. We long for that day, and as his "host of captives," we live by the grace "given to each one of us."

What a glorious paradox: Jesus, our King, didn't triumph over us with a sword but by his cross—by his incomparable humility, not by his unparalleled might. And instead of taking treasure from us, he took our sin from us and gave us his multifaceted grace. Let that sink in.

This is why the humility, gentleness, patience, and loving forbearance mentioned in verse 2 are essential elements of a culture of grace. We're not the good guys fighting the culture (or other Christians). We're grace-people conquered by Jesus. We have a lot to be humble about and grateful for.

Burning incense would often accompany a Roman victory parade. The primary smell associated with the gospel is the aroma of grace (see 2 Corinthians 2:15). I believe that's what Karen smelled those four Sundays during her visit to Christ Community Church. Let's pray that the grace of God will be the most noticeable aroma wafting from our lives, marriages, and churches.

A CULTURE OF SERVING AND EQUIPPING (VV. 11–16)

Servanthood is another essential expression of a culture of grace. The grace we receive from Jesus is always to be shared with others. In union with the consummate Servant, Jesus, we find freedom to live less as takers and more as givers.

Leaders become pacesetters in servanthood. "Apostles, prophets, evangelists, shepherds and teachers" are, like Jesus, to be those among us who serve. When Jesus washed his disciples' feet in the upper room, and then their hearts from the cross, he set the bar very "low" for the leaders he gives to his church. Christ's leaders grab a wash towel quicker than a scepter.

Jesus commissions leaders to equip fellow believers for a life of ministry—in the church, family, and kingdom. He gives saving grace and serving grace to each member of his body. A healthy church isn't a lot of people gathering to hear a few people sing and one person talk. Rather, it's an every-member family, being discipled, equipped, and deployed into service. There are no unnecessary members in the body of Christ.

DISCUSSION *10 MINUTES*

The article mentions six characteristics of a culture of grace: worship, welcome, humility, gratitude, serving, and equipping. What do you find attractive about these characteristics? Is there one that stands out and is especially meaningful to you? Which one, and why?

Imagine what it would look like for the gospel of grace to be the most noticeable aroma wafting from your life, your marriage, and your church. What behaviors would people notice from you? What words would they hear you speak? What would be happening behind the scenes in your life for you to keep these things up?

Lesson

EXERCISE

A CHURCH'S SMELL

20 minutes

For this exercise, you will consider how a culture of grace makes a difference in a church and how people might be able to "smell" that grace culture. Work through the exercise on your own first, and then share some of your results with the group once everyone is ready.

STEP 1: WHAT OUTSIDERS EXPECT TO SENSE IN A CHURCH

Consider some of the non-grace "smells" that we don't want to have in our churches, but might still be there. Note which items outsiders you know might say they would expect to sense if they were to attend a church.

☐ "I might smell a RELIGIOUS SHOW. I expect church people to be more interested in making themselves look good than in making Jesus look good."

☐ "I'd smell a RIP-OFF. Church people want something from me—a convert for their tribe, agreement with their pet views, or my money. They'd rather take than give."

☐ "I'd smell a LAME PARTY. Church people love the church experience, but I'm not into that, and I'm not sure they actually love Jesus—or others."

☐ "I'd smell RELIGIOUS SNOBBERY. Church people think they know better, live better, and deserve better than me."

☐ "I'd smell an UPTIGHT KILLJOY. Everything that seems normal to me seems to bother church people. They even seem bothered by each other, the preacher, and their own church music."

☐ "I'd smell an IN-CROWD. I don't think church people feel that Jesus is for strangers—especially those from different or sinful backgrounds."

☐ Other: _____.

Now, go through that same list a second time. This time, ask yourself which of those non-grace smells you actually might contribute to sometimes—that is, outsiders might sense it from you because you actually get like that. Be honest with yourself. The items probably don't all apply, but it's likely some do. (Be sure to make this part about *you personally*. Don't use it as a way to criticize the whole church or others in your church.)

STEP 2: WHAT A CULTURE OF GRACE DOES FOR A CHURCH

Now consider a second list. This one is some of the "smells" that come with a culture of grace. Note some that you especially wish people would say after coming to church and meeting you.

☐ "I smell a HUMBLE HEART. These people seem to think they are just as undeserving of God as I am—maybe more."

❏ "I smell SERVANTS. Even the leaders don't act better than me or out to get something from me. This sounds crazy, but I think they respect me—despite all my history."

❏ "I smell THANKSGIVING. Not like the holiday where you stuff yourself and show off how much you have, but the kind where you're bowled over by how much you've been given."

❏ "I smell an OPEN DOOR. It seems like anyone can come in. You don't need to get yourself fixed up first."

❏ "I smell TRUE WORSHIP. These people love Jesus and feel they need him, not deserve him."

❏ "I smell LOVE. They aren't just here to sing and get preached at. They're also here to care and be cared for. It's not just about 'Jesus and me,' but about what Jesus wants to do through me for the sake of others."

❏ "I smell REAL PURPOSE. The people here are part of something larger than just their church and their concerns. They are connected to other believers around the world and are doing things to reach those who don't yet know Jesus and make the world a better place."

❏ "I smell HOPE. God is changing people here. Things can be different in my life. I feel free to bring other strugglers who are hungry for the grace I've found here."

❏ Other: _____.

Now share some of your responses with the group. What do outsiders expect from a church, and what does a culture-of-grace church offer that will surprise them in a good way?

What about yourself? How do you most hope to grow to be a more gospel-centered church member? How can a stronger appreciation of all that Jesus has done for you help you be part of a culture of grace?

WRAP-UP AND PRAYER *10 MINUTES*

The path to a culture of grace is not through willpower, but through Jesus. Pray that he will strengthen you in the inner being to be people of grace. Pray also that you would know more and more of his love, for this is where growth tends to start. If you want, you might go back to Ephesians 3:14–19 and use it again as a template for your prayer.

7

REPENTANCE AND GOSPEL TRANSFORMATION

BIG IDEA

The gospel of Jesus and all he does for us creates a culture where change and growth are the norm—where we feel secure enough, confident enough, and thankful enough to openly repent of our selfishness.

BIBLE CONVERSATION *15 minutes*

In chapter 4 of Ephesians, Paul has been describing the unique culture formed when the body of Christ comes together. In today's passage, we will see that it is a culture of ongoing renewal and change. Have a person or two read **Ephesians 4:17–32** aloud, and then discuss the questions below as a group.

Paul presents a stark difference between the old self (mentioned in verse 22) and a believer's new self (mentioned in verse 24). Besides "old vs. new," what are some other contrasts that describe the difference knowing Jesus makes? See if you can pick out several.

Which of these contrasts fits your experience, and how? Where do you see differences between how you were before you started following Christ and afterwards?

This passage presents a two-part process of godly change: we "put off" the old self, and we "put on" the new self. Why is it necessary for us to concentrate on both? What are some examples from your life?

****

Read the article together now, switching readers at the paragraph breaks. Then discuss the questions that follow.

THE HEART OF GOSPEL GROWTH

5 minutes

When Paul describes a culture of grace, he uses the metaphor of walking. Walking presupposes process and journey, not perfection and arrival. A community shaped by the gospel will always be growing in the "double cheer-ups"—the (cheerful!) news that we are more sinful than we realize but still more loved in Christ than we could dare hope. In such a community, no one feels they have arrived. Instead, everyone is discovering more of their need for grace and more of the riches of grace. They won't have less to repent of; rather, they will offer quicker, deeper, and more joyful repentances. Why?

The more we center on Jesus, the more of his beauty and love we discover. This exposes the many ways we are not like the One we are called to reveal—the One we will be like one day. This ever-increasing knowledge of Jesus convicts us. But it doesn't condemn us, because we are already forgiven and righteous in him. We have nothing to prove, just a gospel to believe.

This frees us from our posing and pretending. It frees us for a life of repentance and gospel transformation. Few things compare to the privilege of walking with friends who know how to boast in their weakness and boast in Christ. Everyone becomes a "chief repenter"—leading with vulnerability, humility, and joy. Peers, proteges, and colleagues all find freedom to trust. They can be open about struggles, and grow in grace.

In our passage in Ephesians, Paul gives several concrete examples of how the gospel transforms us. What does growing in grace look like?

Futile thinking is replaced with learning Christ (vv. 17–21). In a culture of grace, we don't just move from wrong thinking to good theology. We "learn Christ"—not just learn about him. The informed mind becomes an inflamed heart, leading to engaged hands. Loving a theology of grace is good, but our real goal is to love the Lord of all grace, Jesus.

The vestiges of our fallen nature are replaced with garments of grace and evidences of new life (vv. 22–24). Paul uses a clothing metaphor—putting off and putting on—to emphasize the dailyness and intentionality of growth. Our progress in Christ is not superficial. We grow from the inside out. Each day we must choose to live more in line with our new nature given to us by Christ and our new identity in Christ.

Dishonest living is replaced with "truthing in love" (v. 25). In a culture of grace, *truthing in love* (the actual Greek phrase), becomes the norm. Not only do we speak honestly to each other, we also live openly and honestly with each other. Anyone can speak the truth, but the gospel must be in play for us to speak the truth in love.

Destructive anger is replaced with redemptive conflict (vv. 26–27). Conflict is inevitable, but good conflict is not. The actual command in this text is, "Be angry, but do not sin." The Bible never tells us not to be angry, but to be careful with the emotion of anger—to steward it carefully. The more time we spend in relationship with anyone, the greater the probability we will disappoint, frustrate, and hurt them. How we deal with these issues is just as important as the issues themselves.

Stealing is replaced with generosity (v. 28). What a profound reversal Paul gives us! In a culture of grace, thieves are redeemed, are trusted with work, and become generous with others. The gospel frees us from all kinds of stealing. Reputation thievery is an example. Gossips become encouragers as they grow in grace.

Speaking to harm is replaced with speaking to heal (v. 29). How we use our words is never merely about tongue control, but heart treasure. Our mouths speak from the overflow of our hearts. When grace is in our hearts, grace is on our lips.

Grieving the Spirit is replaced with the life in the Spirit (v. 30). The Holy Spirit is a person we love, not a force we fear. Think of the last person in the world you would hate to grieve because of their love for you and your love for them. That's close to the image Paul is seeking to convey when he says not to grieve the Spirit. The Holy Spirit applies Jesus to our hearts and tells us how much the Father loves us. Why would we carelessly do and say things that contradict this loving member of the Godhead? Grace motivates and empowers us in ways the law and shame never can.

Bitterness and wrath are replaced with kindness and forgiveness (vv. 31–32). In a culture of grace, it is assumed that we will fail and hurt each other, for we are sinner-saints. But moving toward one another in love becomes the standard, not the exception. Faith expressing itself in love (Galatians 5:6) replaces resent expressing itself in payback. It is God's kindness that leads us to repentance, so where do we think our snarkiness, irritation, and bitterness will lead others? Forgiveness is one of the most non-negotiable, powerful, complex, and challenging callings we share as the people of God. But it's also one of the surest signs that we "get" the gospel and are committed to cultivating a culture of grace.

DISCUSSION *10 MINUTES*

Look back through the article's list of concrete ways the gospel transforms us. Which one most stands out to you, and why? (Perhaps it looks most radical to the world, or is such a praiseworthy change, or is personally meaningful to you, etc.)

Describe the difference between a church culture where everyone feels they have to have arrived at these attitudes already and one that's a journey of growth. What has been your experience with these two different cultures? How do you find the walking metaphor helpful?

POSING AND PRETENDING VS. REPENTING AND BELIEVING

20 minutes

God has called each of us to an entire life of open repentance—admitting, sorrowing over, and turning from sin. This is vastly different from a so-called "Christian" life that's really filled instead with posing and pretending. A truly repentant life is always a believing life too, because only a firm confidence in Christ—and joy in the good news of what we have in him—lets us avoid pretending.

POSING AND PRETENDING

This person is insecure. Their life is based on a need to prove themselves to God, others, or his own conscience. They will be desperate to look better than they are. Whether this ends in pride or despair, they will have little joy in Jesus because they are trying to be their own savior.

REPENTING AND BELIEVING

This person feels secure. Their life is based on what Jesus has done, continues to do, and will complete in them. They are no longer bound to the urge to build any better reputation. They have joy in Jesus and is free to repent and love others.

For this exercise, read through the descriptions of posing and pretending and of repenting and believing. Note some sets that are particularly meaningful to you—places God has helped you to make progress, or places you want more progress. When everyone is ready, discuss the questions at the end together.

Posing and Pretending	Repenting and Believing
I quickly get angry at others, especially if they've made me look bad.	I *have* been bad, but in Jesus I'm a child of the King. No one can touch that reputation. I'm free to forgive in all kinds of situations rather than nurse selfish anger.
I'm slow to admit my mistakes. The vibe you get from me is that other people need to grow, but I don't.	I'm forgiven, and God's ongoing work in me reflects his wise schedule more than my spiritual expertise. I don't mind admitting that I still need to grow much.
I get bitter. If you disregard me or hurt me, I will make sure there's a price to pay.	I don't need to always get my way. My life is already filled to the brim with amazing grace. And being forgiven by God, I forgive others.
I bristle at criticism. I might act like I'm listening to it, but I'm actually building my defense.	I'm forgiven, so criticism doesn't destroy me. It helps me grow, so I'm thankful for it even when it's hard to hear.
When I'm asked to serve, part of my consideration is who will notice and what they will think. I need for someone to notice.	With the constant love and eternal approval of my Father that I have in Jesus, my need for approval from others fades. I can be a true servant.
I'd rather not call it "lying." Let's just say I selectively share the truth to make others think well of me.	My Father sees me through the finished work of Christ. *Christian* is all the good name I need.

Posing and Pretending	Repenting and Believing
Yes, I get cynical. Who wouldn't? Just look at the way some Christians act and some of the oh-so-wrong things they believe!	I have faith that God is at work not only in me but in my fellow believers. I enjoy praising what God is working in them, not criticizing what he has withheld.
I more often point out the sins of others than my own sins. (No, this isn't gossip. I call it "discernment.")	Christ is my reputation. When I feel no further need to build myself up, gossip withers and confession thrives.
The question, "What's in this for me?" is always in the back of my mind.	My God supplies all my needs. I'm free to ask, "What's in this for others?"
My confession of sin is calculated—just enough to make me look humble, not enough to risk anyone looking down on me.	I can be open and honest about my sin because I am secure and loved in my Savior.
I won't admit it, but deep down I realize I've become callous to certain of my sins. I've hidden them for so long that my "struggle" with them is more like a habitual surrender.	I am forgiven and enlisted for battle. In Christ, it is my honor to drag my sin out into the open where I can engage the fight, and where I can receive help.
I rarely talk about Jesus with others who don't know him. I don't want to be known as a "religious nut" or be rejected.	I'm happy to share my own need for Jesus with others, without being pushy or dramatic. I struggle, and I know others do too. Jesus is there for us.
I'm often callous or even angry with those who reject Jesus and live lifestyles that are opposed to his teaching. I may not say anything publicly, but I judge people like this in my heart all the time.	I realize that I too was once a child of wrath and God's enemy. When I hear others reject him, it breaks my heart for them. I'm still a big sinner who in some ways rejects Jesus every day too.

Discuss these questions with the group:

Where has God helped you make progress in your life as a believer in Jesus, giving you deeper belief and repentance? Where do you want more progress? Explain.

It takes practice to grow by faith. How can you start making progress by *believing* the promises of the gospel instead of relying on your own strength and efforts to grow?

- By believing what is done, accomplished, and already true of you in Christ?

- By believing what is happening in you now, by Christ's work in you today?

- By believing what future with Christ is in store for you?

WRAP-UP AND PRAYER *10 MINUTES*

This lesson stressed the importance of believing (faith) in Christian growth and transformation. As you leave, don't make the mistake of thinking faith is something you need to conjure up on your own. Remember how Ephesians 2:8 taught us that faith itself is received: "And this is not your own doing; it is the gift of God." So pray together not only that God would help you to repent, but also that he would increase your faith—your confidence in Jesus and all that you have in him.

Lesson

GOSPEL-FUELED HOLINESS

BIG IDEA

Holiness isn't merely a life of sin management and trying harder. Only the riches of God's grace are sufficient to meet the demands and delights of biblical holiness.

BIBLE CONVERSATION *15 minutes*

As we enter chapter 5 of Ephesians, Paul is in a section of his letter where he describes what kind of life befits a people who know Jesus and Jesus's love. Have someone, or a few readers, read **Ephesians 5:1–20** aloud. Then discuss the questions below:

Paul summarizes God's call to holiness this way: "Be imitators of God, as beloved children. And walk in love, as Christ loved us and gave himself for us." What do you find appealing, or challenging, in that calling and the way it is presented?

Verse 6 says a sinful life lures us with "empty words." What's empty about the call of sin? How do its words compare with the words Paul uses to urge us to live a holy life?

In verses 8–14, what is the difference between darkness and light, and how do they interact? What are some ways these rules of interaction might apply in your daily life?

****

Continue your study of holiness by reading the article. Take turns reading it aloud, and then discuss the questions that follow.

A HOLY LIFE

5 minutes

When you hear the word *holiness*, what images and emotions come to mind? Maybe the word is new to you. Perhaps you think God's grace makes holiness irrelevant. Or maybe you grew up with a healthy understanding of holiness and godliness.

I don't want to project my story (and pain) on you, but my first encounters with the concept of holiness created more fear and doubt than faith and peace. Here's a summary of what I was taught as a young follower of Jesus:

- Holiness is what I must do in response to Jesus's death on the cross. He did his part, now I've got to do my part. I must make myself holy by living a pure and godly life.

- Holiness is keeping God's rules, confessing and grieving and repenting of all my sins, and avoiding future sin. If I live with unconfessed sin, God won't listen to my prayers and he will bring hardship into my life.

- Holiness is what I must have in order to live under the favor of God and have the assurance of heaven. More holiness leads to more blessings from God and greater peace about going to heaven.

Just typing out these memories makes my flesh crawl and my temper flare. Why? Take a close look. None of these statements actually requires Jesus. His death on the cross is assumed, but only as something Jesus did for everybody to make salvation possible for anyone who will get to work.

The problem with much teaching on holiness is that it's not holy enough. Any teaching on godliness, sanctification, and purity that doesn't make Jesus essential and sufficient for the whole process is destructive. And any teaching about holiness that is "doable" apart from the riches of the gospel is evil—that's no exaggeration.

So what *does* the Bible actually mean by *holiness*? Both the Hebrew and Greek words convey the concept of set-apart-ness. Something is holy as it fulfills its original design and purpose.

For instance, I don't make my favorite fly-fishing rod holy by using it to stir paint, take down cobwebs, or wave it as an orchestra baton. Rather, I have set apart my fly-fishing rod for catching nice, big trout. I *sanctify* it (the act of making holy) by using it on lovely rivers in Montana and elsewhere.

Likewise, you and I are holy to the extent we fulfill God's original design and purpose for our lives. Our passage in Ephesians begins with a perfect description of biblical holiness, or set-apart-ness: "Therefore be imitators of God, as beloved children. And walk in love." God designed us to be like him, to live in perfect relationship with himself as his children, and to live a life of love. In summary:

- Holiness is measured by God's perfection, not a dumbed-down version of God's law. "Be imitators of God . . ."
- Holiness means taking on the family likeness. We are beloved children of our Father, destined to be like our elder brother, Jesus. ". . . as dearly loved children."

- Holiness is a life of walking in love—primary love for God, and costly love for others. "And walk in love."

Let this sink in. We are holy to the degree we are imitations of God—not counterfeits, but faithful representations of God's truth, beauty, and goodness. That's how high the standard of biblical holiness actually is. Having been made in the image of God, we are to increasingly reveal his image in the world. We have been made by God, for God, to be like God. This is what Jesus meant when he said, "You therefore must be perfect, as your heavenly Father is perfect" (Matthew 5:48).

The most appropriate thing to ask next is how this is possible. If the holiness God demands isn't an approximate holiness, but a perfect holiness, where can this holiness be acquired? How can we become as perfect as our heavenly Father is perfect? There's only one way. "Christ loved us and gave himself up for us, a fragrant offering and sacrifice to God" (v. 2).

Holiness is grounded in the work of Jesus on our behalf. We're always coming back to the gospel. We cannot hear this too much. Jesus is our substitute to trust before he is our model to follow. Jesus was perfect on our behalf in two ways: he perfectly fulfilled the demands of God's law for us, and he completely exhausted the judgment we deserve.

But what does the practical outworking of our legal righteousness look like? Having been *declared* righteous in Christ, we are now also being *made* righteous by Christ. The writer of Hebrews puts it like this: "For by one sacrifice he has made perfect forever those who are being made holy" (Hebrews 10:14 NIV). We are perfectly forgiven, but we are just starting to be perfected.

We who have been given the legal status of righteous saints (justification) are now growing the righteous nature of God's children (sanctification). That order must never be reversed, but the second must necessarily follow the first. In verses 3–7 of our passage, Paul makes it abundantly clear that if we have zero desire for a life that actually practices holiness, we have no basis to claim that we have been declared holy in the first place. We have no claim to be saved by Jesus's grace.

Holiness is an issue of the affections and direction of the heart. Paul drives home this point by taking on two primary expressions of sin's devastating effect on our hearts: sexual immorality and covetousness (greed). Both of these are so destructive because we are supposed to be imitators of Christ. They cause our lives to lie about the Savior who made us—and remade us in himself. They pillage our calling to love God with everything we have and love our neighbor as ourselves.

Paul calls greed "idolatry"—broken worship. Our uber-generous God made us for a life of contentment, generosity, and thanksgiving. Greed replaces that with discontent, grabbing, and hoarding. Likewise, God made us to steward our sexual longings so that sexual intercourse becomes a symbol of the intimacy, joy, and fellowship of God himself—a good gift for husband and wife. We mock that when we use it for self-pleasure, control, and harm.

Yes, Jesus has taken the wrath for all who trust in him. But those who trust in him take these matters very seriously. And when we do, we become people who "walk as children of light"—both personally and corporately. In union with Jesus, the church offers a small but substantive foretaste of the day when God's glory will fill the earth as the waters cover the sea.

I love how Peter describes our calling: "Live such good lives among the pagans that, though they accuse you of doing wrong, they may see your good deeds and glorify God on the day he visits us" (1 Peter 2:12 NIV). Few things are as inviting, disarming, and beautiful than a local church lit up with the gospel, walking in repentance, growing in grace, and loving its neighbors and community well.

DISCUSSION *10 MINUTES*

What is your gut reaction to the word *holiness*? What wrong or harmful ideas about it have you had, or heard? What do you appreciate about the article's description of the biblical view of holiness?

When you get lax in your seriousness about sexual immorality or greed—or other sin—why does that happen? What has God put in your life that helps keep you serious about holiness?

HOLINESS IN COMMUNITY

20 minutes

We need to take Paul's walking image down to a practical level. Whom do you *really* walk with? With whom are you sharing life the way Paul outlines it? Usually, growth in gospel holiness is nourished and flourishes best in groups smaller than a whole church. A certain kind of close friendship is necessary.

For this exercise, "walk" through Paul's instructions in verses 15–20. Consider how the applications below apply to you. Do you have friends who provide what is described? What part of the description is missing in your life? Work through the exercise on your own first, completing whichever parts apply. When the group is ready, you'll have a chance to share some of your findings if you wish.

WALK WITH THE WISE

"Look carefully then how you walk, not as unwise but as wise" (v. 15).

The wisest friends we can have in life are those who believe Jesus to be "wisdom from God, —that is, our righteousness, holiness and redemption" (1 Corinthians 1:30 NIV). There are many people who are wise in the ways of the world, wise at making money, or wise with pithy sayings. Look for close friends who share your love for Jesus, the gospel, and a life of growing in grace.

I have this in my life because God has given me _____
_____.

In my life, I am missing the part of this that's about having

_____
_____.

MAKE GOSPEL FRIENDSHIPS A SCHEDULE PRIORITY.

"Making the best use of the time, because the days are evil" (v. 16).

This is less about how to get stuff done and much more about how to thrive in life. If we don't make gospel friendships a high priority, they'll simply be crowded out with so many other things. Paul underscores the importance of this commitment by mentioning that the days are evil. Life between the resurrection and return of Jesus is filled with both "good things" that can seduce us and evil things that can destroy us.

I have this in my life because I _____
_____.

In my life, I am missing the part of this that's about having _____
_____.

WALK TOGETHER IN THE SPIRIT.

"Be filled with the Spirit" (v. 18).

Paul offers a striking contrast between living under the influence of alcohol and living under the invigorating influence of the Holy Spirit. There is no holiness without the work of the Spirit. Gospel friendships will make time for the holy, Spirit-led tasks of confessing sins to each other, repenting together with joy, being open about weakness and brokenness, bearing each other's burdens, serving others, and praying together.

I have this in my life because God has given me _____

_____.

In my life, I am missing the part of this that's about having _____

_____.

PREACH THE GOSPEL TO OURSELVES AND EACH OTHER.

"Addressing one another in psalms and hymns and spiritual songs" (v. 19).

This certainly is good instruction for maturing the worship culture of a church. But at a more micro-level, it's a great way to think about the discipline of preaching the gospel to ourselves and then to each other. The best thing we can do for any of our relationships is to continually study the whole story of God (psalms, hymns, and spiritual songs) from Genesis through Revelation, discovering how Jesus is the only true hero and the Yes to every promise God has made. This will lead us to "singing and making melody to the Lord" in our hearts, and "giving thanks always and for everything to God the Father in the name of our Lord Jesus Christ." The most transforming relationships are filled with Spirit-fullness, Christ-awe, and Father-gratitude.

I have this in my life because God has given me _____

_____.

In my life, I am missing the part of this that's about having ____
_____.

WALK IN GOSPEL-ACCOUNTABILITY.

"Submitting to one another out of reverence for Christ."

Gospel friendships are marked by the right kind of accountability. Some accountability groups end up being set-ups for pride, lying, and a fall. The main thing we need to hold each other accountable for is believing the gospel and applying it to every area of life. This leads to a healthy submission to each other in mutual care, not grace-lacking control.

I have this in my life because God has given me _____
_____.

In my life, I am missing the part of this that's about having ____
_____.

When you're done, share with the group the parts you want to talk about. How has God blessed you with others? How do you long for better gospel-centered relationships? What keeps you from those relationships?

WRAP-UP AND PRAYER *10 MINUTES*

If there are blessings of gospel community you long for but don't yet have, pray that God would give those to you and would give you the desire to pursue them.

GOSPEL-SHAPED MARRIAGE

BIG IDEA

God intends marriage to be a reenactment of the gospel designed to reveal the beauty of Jesus and his incomparable love for his bride, the church. Out of reverence for Jesus, a husband and wife are to extend his great love—the love of our ultimate spouse—to each other.

BIBLE CONVERSATION *10 minutes*

Having explained how God's people live in a holy way that fits the gospel, Paul's letter to the Ephesians now addresses how key relationships among believers also should fit the gospel. Paul begins with the marriage relationship. It's possible you've heard many views of how this passage should apply within marriages. But before you discuss that, first complete the Bible conversation to understand what the passage says, and read the article.

Have someone read **Ephesians 5:21–33** aloud. Then discuss the questions as a group.

What is the basis for the teaching that wives should submit to their husbands? Whom is the wife acting like when she does so?

Considering whom she is acting like, what status, honors, responsibilities, challenges, or other traits define her when she submits?

What is the basis for the teaching that husbands should love their wives? Whom is the husband acting like when he loves his wife? Considering whom he is acting like, what honors, responsibilities, challenges, or other traits define him when he loves his wife?

Now consider husbands and wives together. What story are they reenacting? What honors and responsibilities come with reenacting that story?

****

Now read through the article together, taking turns reading aloud by paragraph. When you finish, discuss the questions at the end.

Lesson

ARTICLE

SUBMITTING AND LOVING OUT OF REVERENCE

10 minutes

I was clueless about many things when Darlene and I got married in 1972. The first night I met Darlene, I sensed she might just be the one. But because I felt she was out of my league, I didn't ask her out until after a year-long brother/sister-in-Christ relationship. Two or three dates later, I proposed marriage. We became Mr. and Mrs. Scotty Smith after a whopping three-month engagement. Our premarital counseling consisted of a single, one-hour session. But for the grace of God . . .

Indeed, God has been incredibly patient, tenacious, and kind to us over our forty-seven years of married life. Our most important growth as a couple has taken place after the twenty-five-year mark. I hope that encourages some of you who may be in a difficult season. I shake my head in disbelief at how ill-prepared Darlene and I were for marriage at the start, and how little we understood about the true meaning of Christian marriage. We wanted to do it right, so we studied our roles—but we missed the point.

At the time, we believed my role was to be the spiritual leader—the "head of my household," executing loving authority over my wife. Darlene was to be a submissive wife, quietly trusting God when we disagreed and patiently waiting when I was in error. But think about it. This version of a Christian marriage doesn't require Jesus, disregards the centrality of the gospel, and makes relationship with a human spouse more the issue than relationship with our ultimate spouse, Christ.

So what *does* this text from Ephesians actually teach about marriage, and what are the implications of this passage not just for spouses, but for everyone? Many Bible teachers struggle to decide whether verse 21, "submitting to one another out of reverence for Christ," is the conclusion of Paul's preceding section on life in the body of Christ or the introduction to his reflections on Christian marriage. I don't think it's an either/or issue. I believe Paul strategically included this statement right in the middle of a wider conversation about all kinds of relationships for those who are in Christ.

Reverence for Jesus is to be the defining reality in all of our relationships—in the church, family, and culture. The more we revere Jesus, the more we will live for his glory, and by his grace, in each of our relationships. We revere Jesus when we affectionately adore and submit to him—when we have a fitting response to who he is and what he has done for us in the gospel. The more we experience Jesus's beauty and glory and grace and love, the more we will extend these riches to others. By God's design, when the gospel is the primary story shaping marriage, the husband and wife each reveal different dimensions of the love of Jesus to each other.

WIVES AND THE SUBMISSIVE HEART OF JESUS

Notice that Paul doesn't instruct wives to submit to their husbands as their lord, but *as unto the Lord.* There's a world and gospel of difference between the two. A wife's primary submission (like that of her husband) is to Jesus. Her submission to Jesus qualifies her submission to her husband—its nature and limits. This passage doesn't call for absolute, unquestioned obedience, for only Jesus deserves that allegiance. Nor does it mean the husband makes all the decisions and the wife is an unthinking responder.

Too often, men have used this passage as an excuse to act sinfully toward women or treat them as people to boss around. That's never okay, and it is not what this passage teaches. Rather, a husband is called to be a servant-leader whose headship is less about authority and more about responsibility for his wife. The fact that Paul connects Jesus's headship of the church with his being its Savior underscores the grace dynamics of a husband's headship.

Indeed, in her submission, a wife models the church's submission to Jesus—a point of major significance in this passage. The primary metaphor here is Jesus's relationship as the perfect bridegroom to his grace-needy bride, the church. Jesus is the spouse we always wanted—the ultimate spouse to whom we are more married than we will ever be to a human spouse.

In fact, the only marriage that will last throughout eternity is the marriage between Jesus and his church. We won't live as married couples in the new heaven and new earth (see Matthew 22:30). That makes this text just as relevant to single Christians. Every believer is married to Jesus.

The temporary nature of earthly marriages makes them more important, not less. There's limited time to reenact an important story God wants to tell through marriage. A wife's submission to her husband reveals a glimpse of the submission Jesus gave our heavenly Father throughout his incarnate life. Jesus is the consummate example of loving submission. The cross was the most difficult submission Jesus offered his Father, but it was also the greatest expression of his love for us. Mutual submission in every gospel-shaped relationship flows from the finished work of Jesus's cross and is part of the ongoing work of the cross in our lives.

HUSBANDS AND THE SACRIFICIAL LOVE OF JESUS

Jesus's love for his bride is the quintessential example of sacrificial love, and that's the kind of love a Christian husband is called to offer his wife. Far from proclaiming his authority and demanding her submission, a gospel-captured husband chooses the cross, not a throne, to define his relationship with his wife. Jesus gave himself up for his bride, and a husband is called to do the same for his wife—even to the point of death.

Paul mentions several expressions of Jesus's love for the church that have a parallel in a marriage shaped by the gospel. The gospel calls a husband to reveal the other-centered honoring, refreshing, nourishing, and cherishing love of Jesus. A husband isn't called to fix or change his wife, but to prepare her for life with her ultimate spouse. A loving husband can be an extension of the transforming, healing grace of the gospel, though not its replacement.

The preoccupation and attention a husband naturally might have for himself is to be channeled instead toward his wife. This is what Paul means by calling a husband to love his wife as his own body. The image is rooted in the daily care each of us shows in bathing, grooming, and clothing ourselves. We must not take each other for granted, or ignore daily needs, or withhold intentional acts of kindness.

But even more, Paul wants us to live with a stunned awareness that this is the way Jesus nourishes and cherishes us as his bride. His mercies are new every morning because we need the mercies of Jesus every day. This is the love that also should increasingly define life in the local church and be revealed to those in our communities.

JESUS OUR MODEL

We may be tempted to look at how husbands and wives are given different instructions and wonder which is the greater role, or how we can preserve our rights. But this completely misses the point. To Paul, *both* roles come with greatness because they replay the gospel story of Christ and the church. And that greatness is the lowly kind modeled by Jesus, where we give up our rights and our very selves for the sake of our spouse.

Wives make themselves lowly by submitting as unto the Lord. Husbands make themselves lowly by loving as Christ loved the church. In the Bible, Christ-like love means putting the needs of others first by taking the low place: Jesus "emptied himself, taking the form of a servant" (Philippians 2:7), and he "came not to be served but to serve, and to give his life as a ransom for many" (Mark 10:45). Christian wives and Christian husbands *both* practice lowliness for the sake of the other. *That* is what makes a Christian marriage different—and glorious.

The Bible begins and ends with a marriage, so it shouldn't surprise us that Paul concludes this section hearkening back to the first marriage between Adam and Eve. But what is truly astonishing is that he says the whole event was about Jesus and the church.

Jesus left his Father and the glory that was eternally his. He lived in our place and died in our place to make a most unlikely and ill-deserving people his wife and queen. Jesus cleaves to us with covenant love, has robed us in the wedding garment of his own righteousness, and is coming back for us—bridegroom for beloved bride. An eternity of intimacy with Jesus defines us forever as the bride of Christ. How can we not revere so great a Savior? May our marriages and churches more faithfully tell this greatest of all true stories.

DISCUSSION *15 MINUTES*

What are some ideas you've held about marriage that may be missing the main point? Explain.

Think about the ways you submit to Jesus and the honor that comes from giving up your own demands for his sake. What are some day-to-day ways you can reenact that kind of submission either in your role as a wife (if you are one) or in some other relationship?

Think about the ways Jesus gave up himself for us, to present us holy before God, and the honor that comes from laying down your own life in a similar way. What are some day-to-day ways you can reenact Jesus's dying to self in your role as a husband (if you are one) or in some other relationship?

Lesson

EXERCISE

REVERENCE FOR JESUS

15 minutes

We've seen that gospel relationships start with reverence for Jesus. Sadly, many of us think of reverence more like rigor mortis than resurrection life—as if reverence meant being afraid of God. It actually means seeing clearly who Jesus is and adoring him for it.

For this exercise, you'll start by noticing truths about Jesus that produce reverence in you. From there, you'll move into what this means for your relationships. For that part, think in terms of your spouse if you're married, or of some other close relationship if you aren't. Work through the exercise on your own first. You'll be able to share some of your responses later.

STEP 1: HOW YOU REVERE JESUS

Begin by thinking of some things you find most amazing and worship-worthy about Jesus. The possibilities are nearly endless, from the way he looked at people with compassion to how he will wield the sword as King of kings. Think of up to three things that make you marvel.

I revere Jesus because he _____

_____.

I revere Jesus because he _____
_____.

I revere Jesus because he _____
_____.

STEP 2: HOW YOUR HEART REACTS

Reverence produces wide-ranging emotions. Note some that fit
how you tend to revere Jesus.

- ☐ Amazed astonishment

- ☐ Unspeakable joy

- ☐ Thankful repentance

- ☐ Knee-buckling awe

- ☐ Face-down quiet

- ☐ David-like dancing

- ☐ Silent contemplation

- ☐ Searching wonder

- ☐ Comforting hope

- ☐ Steadfast love

- ☐ Other: _____

STEP 3: YOUR RELATIONSHIP

An emotional life grounded in Jesus will change your approach to
your spouse or other relationship. Read through each description
and note how true it is of you.

When I revere Jesus MORE, he fills my emotional needs.

- Instead of concerning myself over what emotional satisfaction I get out of my relationship, I can accept and even celebrate the "lowly like Jesus" role God calls me to fulfill.
- I respect and care for the other person.
- I have an overflow of emotional energy to give.
- My relational style is one of neither superiority nor inferiority, but rather gospel humility.
- The act of giving (which could include things like submitting, respecting, loving) is to me a way to worship Jesus—so it doesn't just drain me, it also refills me.

This is true of me (pick one): SELDOM / SOMETIMES / OFTEN

When I revere Jesus LESS, I begin to look to my spouse (or other relationship) to give me what Jesus alone can truly provide.

- I am more concerned with my relationship being right for me than I am with me being right with God.
- I get frustrated that my relationship isn't filling my needs.
- I am more of a taker than I am a giver (or I get focused on which of us is taking/giving the most).
- My God-given role in the relationship feels like a burden to bear rather than a gospel reenactment to celebrate.

This is true of me (pick one): SELDOM / SOMETIMES / OFTEN

When the group is ready, share some of your results. What is God teaching you about marriage or about Christian relationships in general? Where do you want to grow? How will you make reverence for Jesus a part of that?

WRAP-UP AND PRAYER *10 MINUTES*

No doubt, the difficulties of relationships are much of the reason Paul included his impassioned prayer for the Ephesians to always be growing in their knowledge and experience of the love of Jesus (3:14–21). Make sure your prayers together include not only requests for better relationships, but requests that you would see and revere Jesus better.

Lesson

10

HOME LIFE TRANSFORMED BY GRACE

BIG IDEA

The gospel claims and transforms all our relationships, including how we relate to our parents and our children.

BIBLE CONVERSATION *15 minutes*

In this section of Ephesians, Paul helps us understand the implications of the gospel for a wide range of relationships. He presents the gospel as the third way—avoiding the extremes of both grace-less conservatism and law-less liberalism. "Faith expressing itself in love" becomes the model we want to learn and cultivate in every relationship—including the relationships between parents and children.

Have someone read **Ephesians 6:1–4** aloud. Then discuss the questions below:

Paul instructs children not simply to obey their parents, but to obey them "in the Lord." How might that insert some wiggle room into the instruction? In what ways might it also make the instruction more challenging, not less?

Obeying parents is coupled with the commandment to honor them. Which do you feel is the more difficult instruction to follow, obeying or honoring? Why?

Fathers are told to bring up their children in the discipline and instruction "of the Lord." How might that be different from bringing up your children in your own discipline and instruction? Think of several differences.

Lesson

ARTICLE

CHILDREN AND PARENTS "IN THE LORD"

5 minutes

"That's right, obey your parents, *period*. You don't want to risk the peril of getting out from under your parents' covering of protection. They're not always right, but they're always your parents, and they're God's appointed means of keeping you out of the devil's grasp. And parents, if you do what I'm telling you, there's a greater chance your children will be virgins when they get married, won't mess with drugs and alcohol, and may very well grow up to become missionaries."

I trust you saw the quotation marks framing that opening paragraph. That's certainly not my voice, and it's not an actual quote, but it's scary-close to the kind of family-life teaching Darlene and I heard early in our marriage and parenting. O the burden (curse and evil) of gospel-less, performance-based, formula-laden family life.

I began my journey as a dad more driven by fear than faith, with a greater bent toward protecting our kids *from* the world than preparing them to live *in* the world. As the grace of God became more real to me, I repented but overcorrected. I rejected legalistic pragmatism for a more progressive, laid-back parenting approach. I now grieve both of my approaches.

As we move into this text about parents and children, it's important to remember the context. Paul is still expanding on the beginning of chapter 5, "Therefore be imitators of God, as beloved children. And walk in love, as Christ loved us and gave himself up for us, a fragrant offering and sacrifice to God." So how do beloved children of God live a life of love in response to Jesus's finished work on our behalf? What are the implications of the gospel for parent-child relationships—whether we've grown up in healthy or hellish homes?

THE GOSPEL AND RELATING TO OUR PARENTS

Paul begins this section reminding us of the fifth commandment: each of us is called to obey and honor our father and mother. Of course, there are adjustments for age, stage of life, and the situation in which God has put us. But the gospel doesn't replace the Ten Commandments. Rather, it reclaims their proper meaning and reveals their fullest meaning. To obey, in the original languages of the Bible, means to "place oneself under and listen." Our relationship to our parents is to be marked by servanthood and learning—in every season of the relationship.

Paul assumes the parents he's writing to want to teach their young children critical things about life and God. There are, of course, exceptions—and some of you are painfully marked by those exceptions. This is a way the phrase *in the Lord* qualifies what obeying our parents means, especially as we get older. Paul isn't saying we only have to obey and honor parents who are believers. Rather, we are to obey "as unto the Lord"—that is, with regard to our ultimate parent, God himself. Only our Father has the right to define our relationship with our earthly parents.

Perhaps this helps us understand why the text mentions both obedience and honoring. We are never called to blind obedience, especially when a parent would require us to violate our conscience or break the law. And none of us is called to relate to our parents simply on the basis of *their* definition of honor—serving their efforts to build their own reputation or to control us. Rather, we are called to love and serve our parents in step with the truth of the gospel. In many ways, that is more demanding than legalism and codependency. Loving well—whether it's our parents, kids, spouse, neighbors, or friends—always requires more than we want to give, something other than what they demand, and everything God promises to give us.

Jack Miller used to tell me, "Scotty, one of the signs you're growing in grace will be seen in terms of who are you willing to disappoint." Pleasing the Lord and pleasing our parents may be at odds with each another. This is especially true for those of us with difficult family-of-origin stories. Paul says it is *right* to obey and honor our parents—not that it's easy, nor that everything will work out the way we want it to, nor that our love will always be reciprocated.

The fifth commandment was never meant to be understood legalistically or selfishly, that if you want to enjoy the good life for a long time you should be an obedient kid. Rather, family solidarity was going to be essential for Israel's survival as they moved into the hostile land of Canaan, and the promise of a good and long life was a general promise for the whole family. The land we now live in as Christians is our Father's world, and the good life we most care about is our new life in Christ. Our best reason for offering appropriate obedience to God, our parents, or anyone else is because we have already received eternal life and the riches of God's grace. It is not to get anything, but because we have received all things in Christ.

THE GOSPEL AND RELATING TO OUR CHILDREN

Keeping his focus on the home, Paul next addresses parents. Here he specifically addresses fathers because of the crucial role they play in setting the culture of a household, though the same also applies to mothers in this regard. As parents, the attitude with which we parent is just as formative (perhaps more so) as the rules, boundaries, discipline, and instruction we give our children. So Paul warns against provoking our children to anger—fueling shame, fear, or a sense of not measuring up. (This doesn't mean that every time our kids get angry it's a parental failure. Like us, our children are being selfish sometimes.)

The gospel calls parents to identify the idols of our hearts that often lurk behind our harshness, our expectations, and the pressure we put on our children to perform—as students, athletes, artists, Christians, or representatives of our families. We are to parent as unto the Lord, not to get a re-do on life through our kids. Our children are God's inheritance, not our penance. They are made in God's image, not for our reputation or glory.

Parenting is exhausting, glorious, frustrating, and wonderful. That's why our preoccupation must be with bringing our children up "in the discipline and instruction of the Lord." Think of that as teaching our children the lyric, music, and dance of the gospel.

Our children need the content of the gospel—its *lyric*. In keeping with everything Paul has been saying in Ephesians, this will involve a gospel village: our input as parents, the influence of a good local church, good friends, and other gospel-sane adults God brings into their lives. As parents, we can only feed our children what we have in our own heart-refrigerators. Do we know what the Bible actually says about Jesus—his person, work, and will? Do we read the Bible looking for Jesus everywhere? Is engagement in a local church, and sitting under the ministry of the Word, a priority for us? Are we actively fulfilling our role in God's mission by working to see his kingdom grow?

Our kids will hear the *music* of the gospel as they see God's grace at work in our own lives. Is grace vital and sweet to us, or just an important theological category? Is Jesus our heart-treasure or a religious add-on? Do we love others who don't look like us and act like us, or is our faith an "us vs. them" expression of religiosity? Is it easy for us to repent in front of our kids? Do they see the gospel at work between us as spouses—as we humble ourselves, repent, and reconcile? When's the last time our children heard us say to them, "I am so sorry. I missed your heart and dumped my anger and fear on you. Please forgive me."

Lastly, our children will learn the *dance* of the gospel—its rhythms and lifestyle—as they observe our lives. We too are living under the discipline of the Lord—the claims, beauty, and love of Jesus. Think of discipline primarily as formation, not punishment. Of course, we must teach our kids obedience and the consequences of rebellion, and appropriate punishments are part of this process. But proactively, discipline shapes our values, fuels our joy, and establishes our priorities. The dance of the gospel is a missional lifestyle in which Jesus changes the price tags in our hearts, programs the GPS of our lives, and grants us grace to live to his glory. May our children catch us in the process of becoming freer and more like Jesus, so our words about him are more than empty symbols.

DISCUSSION *10 MINUTES*

Describe your approach to your relationship with your parents, or with others in authority over you. What about it honors them, or fails to honor them? What makes it difficult to honor them, and how have you responded to that difficulty?

What parenting approaches have you tried (and perhaps rejected), or what approaches were tried on you? How is gospel parenting different from these?

Lesson

EXERCISE

OUR FATHER AND OUR PARENTING

20 minutes

To be a gospel parent, you first need to be a gospel child of your own Father in heaven. Then you can engage in good parenting because you have experienced it from your good Father. And your children will be most likely to let you parent them because they have watched you let your Father parent you.

On your own, read through the descriptions of how God parents us, his children, and what these mean for our parenting of our children. Note some that are particularly meaningful to you. Perhaps you have experienced and practiced them, or they help you see how your life as a child of God and your parenting could be transformed. If you are not a parent, the exercise will help you prepare for parenthood or for building up any other believers in the faith, which we all should be doing. When the group is ready, discuss the questions at the end of the exercise.

PATIENCE

God's parenting: My Father is exceedingly patient and forgiving toward me even though I repeatedly fail to trust and obey him. "For you, O Lord, are good and forgiving, abounding in steadfast love to all who call upon you" (Psalm 86:5).

My parenting: I realize my child has the same rebellious and fearful sin nature I have, and I patiently train him to find help and mercy in Jesus, as I have.

INSTRUCTION

God's parenting: My Father teaches his children to bear a family resemblance, becoming "blameless and innocent, children of God without blemish" (Philippians 2:15). I am constantly in school with him, learning what that means and how to practice it. "Gather the people to me, that I may let them hear my words, so that they may learn to fear me all the days that they live on the earth, and that they may teach their children so" (Deuteronomy 4:10).

My parenting: I regularly point my kids to God's teaching. My instruction is not first of all about them learning what I say, but about both of us learning what God says. "All your children shall be taught by the LORD, and great shall be the peace of your children" (Isaiah 54:13).

INVOLVEMENT

God's parenting: My Father protects me and provides for me, but best of all he is with me in all circumstances. "For my father and my mother have forsaken me, but the LORD will take me in" (Psalm 27:10).

My parenting: I make time for my child and am involved in her life, demonstrating as best I can how our Father is beside us always.

COMPASSION

God's parenting: My Father cares for me and I am confident that he always does what is right for me—even at great cost to himself. "As a father shows compassion to his children, so the LORD shows compassion to those who fear him" (Psalm 103:13).

My parenting: Secure in my own Father's love, my parenting is free to be motivated by my child's good—not by how my child can please me or make me look good, or how he has disappointed or frustrated me.

LISTENING

God's parenting: I have the privilege of bringing all my needs to my Father—even those that reflect my own failure. When I am worried or fearful or need to confess sin, he gives comfort and forgiveness. "The LORD is near to the brokenhearted and saves the crushed in spirit" (Psalm 34:18).

My parenting: My security rests in my forgiveness and my Father's care, not my child's performance. So I am not prone to scold or lecture when my child confesses sin, experiences failure, or has anxiety. I celebrate a contrite heart.

DISCIPLINE

God's parenting: My Father powerfully and wisely brings hard things into my life at times—to train me in love, not punish me out of spite. "Endure hardship as discipline; God is treating you as his children" (Hebrews 12:7 NIV).

My parenting: I am willing and unafraid to discipline my child when necessary. I do it out of love for her and with her interests in mind, not out of frustration or to assert my superiority, and in the posture of an under-authority who must submit to my own Father's discipline.

PURSUIT

God's parenting: My Father pursues his wayward children when they turn away from him. He is eager to welcome them home. "How can I give you up, O Ephraim? How can I hand you over, O Israel? . . . my compassion grows warm and tender" (Hosea 11:8).

My parenting: I do not lose hope when my child turns away from what I have taught him. My own Father has had wayward children too, and I continue to point my child to him.

HEART-CENTEREDNESS

God's parenting: My Father brings me to himself with my whole person, working firm faith and heartfelt repentance inside of me, not mere good-looking behavior on the outside. "Return to the Lord your God, you and your children, and obey his voice in all that I command you today, with all your heart and with all your soul" (Deuteronomy 30:2).

My parenting: I don't push my child to conform outwardly for my benefit; I urge her to come to Jesus for her benefit, and I look for evidence of inward change.

LOVING OTHERS

God's parenting: My Father loves me so much that he was willing to send Jesus to the cross rather than live without me because of my sin and guilt. My Father now gives me the chance to introduce others to him as I come to him everyday to meet my needs and heal my brokenness. "This is love: not that we loved God, but that he loved us and sent his Son as an atoning sacrifice for our sins" (1 John 4:10 NIV).

My Parenting: I want my children to know that God doesn't just love them, he loves everyone. By coming to God to meet their needs every day, they also have the opportunity to point others to Jesus so that they too can know him.

FAMILY BUILDING

God's parenting: My Father's great mission toward my family is to bring us into his family, "to gather into one the children of God who are scattered abroad" (John 11:52).

My parenting: My goal for my child is not to make him a well-behaved, loyal, and prosperous part of my family, but for him and all of us to be included in God's family.

INHERITANCE

God's parenting: Because God is my Father, I am an heir of eternal life and all its blessings. This is my great hope for my future. "We are children of God, and if children, then heirs—heirs of God and fellow heirs with Christ" (Romans 8:16–17).

My parenting: When I think of my child's future, I mostly think well beyond this life. My hope is not in pushing, prodding, or begging my child to be "successful" here, but in showing her the beauty of Jesus and eternal life in him.

Now share some of your thoughts with the group. Which items already fit your parenting or the way you build up others in the faith? Which do you struggle with? How would you like God to make you more of a gospel child of your Father so you can be more of a gospel parent?

WRAP-UP AND PRAYER *10 MINUTES*

Prayer too is an essential part of both godly parenting and godly honor toward parents. In your closing time together, pray for your children, pray for your parents, and pray for yourselves in your roles as gospel-believing parents and gospel-believing children.

NOTE: If, like many parents, you feel you have irreparably blown it as a dad or mom, I encourage you to read the book *Come Back, Barbara* (Phillipsburg, NJ: P&R, 1997). It's a beautiful dialogue between authors C. Jack Miller and his daughter, Barbara Miller Juliani, reflecting on their painful disconnect earlier in life and how the gospel brought them both to repentance, freedom, and restoration years later as adults. The gospel deserves and gets the last word.

11

WORKING AS UNTO THE LORD

BIG IDEA

The gospel transformation of all our relationships extends into our workplaces, where both workers and bosses should do their jobs with sincere hearts, mindful of Jesus.

BIBLE CONVERSATION *15 minutes*

NOTE: Some English Bibles translate the Greek word *doulos* in this passage as "slave." The evil of slavery as practiced in many places and times in the world clearly does not fit Paul's gospel and we must figure he surely would have severe criticism for the kind of race-based, chattel slavery that existed, for example, in the early years of the United States. But in studying this passage, we should realize that slavery in the Roman Empire during Paul's time was different. Although some masters could be harsh, most slaves were paid and able eventually to buy their freedom. Slaves might own property and be given much responsibility. The New Testament uses *doulos* more than a hundred times, and many of these are references to people entrusted to manage large amounts of wealth or sent on important missions for their masters or for God. In this passage, the ESV is careful to translate *doulos* as "bondservant" so that modern readers will understand this difference. And for the purposes of our discussion, we will treat a *doulos* as similar to a present-day employee, since this is one of the relationships in our world today that probably comes closest to what Paul had in mind.

Paul has written about how the gospel transforms the way we live in all of life, both within and outside of the church. In this section of his letter, he has written specifically about submission in husband-wife and parent-child settings. Now he addresses boss-worker settings, which in Ephesus may have typically been extensions of home life.

Have someone read **Ephesians 6:5–9** aloud. Then discuss the questions below. (If you don't do vocational work, apply the questions to some other workplace-like setting in your life. It could be a teacher-student, coach-player, ministry leader-worker, or other setting that involves levels of authority.)

What does it look like to obey your boss "with a sincere heart, as you would Christ"? How is that different from the approach people tend to take to obeying their bosses? (Look for answers in the text, and also consider your experience with workplaces.)

Compare the rewards bosses assume we work for with the rewards Paul says we ought to work for. How do they differ, and how might they affect the way you do your particular work?

What might change about the way bosses treat their workers when the bosses remember that both they and their workers have the same Master in heaven?

****

Now read aloud the article, "The Gospel in the Workplace," switching readers at each paragraph break. Then discuss the questions that follow it.

THE GOSPEL IN THE WORKPLACE

It's important to understand that when Paul wrote Ephesians, slavery in Roman culture had already undergone significant change. For sure, many Christians were still living out the horrors of the worse forms of slavery. But others were able to purchase their way out of slavery and worked as hired hands and servants of wealthier families.

Moving from Paul's world into ours, we must acknowledge, grieve, and seek to heal the tragic history of slavery in the United States and around the world. The active participation in slavery by many Christians in the American church, the way that that society created a narrative of racial difference to maintain slavery and racial discrimination, and the guilty silence of those who passively ignored this evil, must not be denied or minimized. There is no systemic expression of sin more glaring in America's history than racism, and though slavery became illegal, racism continues. The gospel Paul preached decries and deconstructs every expression of racism, tribalism, and nationalism.

So, it is likely that here Paul is not addressing settings as sinful as those. He is writing about settings that are closer to workplaces, and he wants to make a point about how we relate to authority as we work. His aim is to show how our primary and lasting relationship with God ought to have a profound impact on our temporary relationships in our earthly workplaces, especially between people who have different degrees of authority and autonomy.

Gospel relationships extend beyond the church and the immediate family. Paul helps us think through the implications of the gospel for the marketplace and our vocational life. In doing so, he connects us with both Eden and our coming life in the new heaven and new earth. When we have a proper view of both creation and the new creation, we will understand the privilege, gift, and goodness of work.

In Eden, Adam and Eve were equally commissioned to fill the earth with God's glory. Theologians refer to this calling as the creation mandate. God appointed human beings to make their whole lives worshipful service, living as stewards of God's world while exercising loving dominion and creating culture. And after Jesus returns, heaven will be no less dynamic, creative, and vocational.

Through the intrusion of sin and death, work came under the curse of God's judgment. Thorns and sweat, pain and frustration became stains on our creative calling. We exchanged stewardship for ownership. We swapped working for the common good with working for "my success." We traded serving our neighbor for exploiting and owning our neighbor.

But now in Christ, that which was lost is being regained. Jesus has come, as we sing in Isaac Watts's "Joy to the World," to make his blessings flow far as the curse is found. When Jesus said, "The Son of Man came not to be served but to serve, and to give his life as a ransom for many" (Matthew 20:28), he was announcing the arrival of his kingdom—a kingdom that will eventually make all things new. He was also demonstrating that leaders and followers are all called to be servants. Humility isn't the way to greatness, it *is* greatness.

Before the day of all things new, Christian employees and employers are both called to demonstrate the breaking in of the kingdom of God and the transforming power of the gospel. "Bondservants" are to obey their masters with appropriate respect and care, working with a good heart, knowing Jesus is our *real* boss. We serve the Servant of all, who also is the Ruler of the kings of the earth.

What Paul teaches has implications for each of us in our vocations. Whether we love our jobs, endure them, or despise them, and whether we're working for the nicest employer possible or the worse narcissist imaginable, we are to do our jobs with excellence. We are to work with all our hearts and with good attitudes—not as people-pleasers, but as Christ-lovers.

Paul says Jesus will reward us, both now and at his return. He will not pay us the wages due us, but lavish us with grace we could never earn. And should Jesus reward us with "crowns," we know the destination of every crown. They will all be cast joyfully at Jesus's feet (Revelation 4:10).

As it does with workers, the gospel also rewires "masters." Bosses are to be grace-filled leaders, not threatening overlords. No servant is greater than his master, and our Master made himself the quintessential Servant. All Christian employers, leaders, or bosses must regularly ask themselves a series of important questions:

- Does my leadership reflect the servant love of Jesus?
- Do I treat my employees and/or staff with equal respect, care, and fairness?
- Would I want to work for me?

- How am I working to break down the economic barriers, power imbalances, and social segregation that often exist in the workplace?

- Since God's kindness leads me to repentance, where should I expect my irritation, gruffness, and lack of kindness to lead my employees and staff?

- Do I position myself in the company as one who serves? Or do I position myself as one who is powerful, most important, and must be celebrated?

Paul's letter to Philemon is a powerful demonstration of the power of the gospel to take hold of people who are in charge over others, inhabiting and transforming social structures and relationships. Paul asks his wealthy friend, Philemon, to welcome back a runaway slave, Onesimus—not as a slave, but now as his brother in Christ. Philemon had a legal right to put Onesimus to death, but Paul challenges him instead to share with his slave the joys of eternal life. Whether we are bosses or busboys, may we aim to join in similar stories of gospel transformation.

DISCUSSION

In your work, what difference does it make when you approach your job as reclaiming work's original design—practicing humility, being a steward, seeking the common good, etc.?

What insights from the article can immediately apply to you in your work, whether as one who answers to others or one who has authority over others?

Lesson

EXERCISE

A WORKPLACE SELF-QUESTIONNAIRE

The questions for yourself that are mentioned in the article can help you see how well you are applying these gospel truths in the workplace. They can also help you want to do better. This exercise adapts those questions into some you can answer and discuss right now. Pick either the set for those under authority or the one for those in authority, and work through the answers on your own. If, like many people, you are both under authority and in authority, pick the set you most want to work on—or answer some of each. If you don't do vocational work, think of some other work-like relationship in your life and apply the questions to that. When you finish, you'll be able to share some of your responses with the group.

QUESTIONS FOR THOSE UNDER AUTHORITY

1. Is my heart attitude one of obedience and submission, like it is with Jesus?

☐ Yes

☐ No

☐ Sometimes

In what situations? _____

_____

2. Do I go about my work as a God-pleaser who is secure in Christ, not as an insecure or scheming people-pleaser?

❏ Yes

❏ No

❏ Sometimes

In what way? _____

_____

3. If I were the boss, would I be thankful for me as a worker?

❏ Yes

❏ No

❏ Sometimes

Why or why not? _____

_____

4. Which is true more often?

❏ My willingness and respect make people want to assign me tasks and willing to correct me when needed.

❏ My irritation makes people cringe at having to assign me tasks or correct me.

Which is true more often?

❏ I position myself as one who serves.

❏ I position myself as one who deserves more recognition for all I do.

In what way? _____

_____

5. Which is most likely true?

❏ My coworkers would say I bring respect, cheerfulness, and a concern for others to the workplace.

❏ My coworkers would say I bring disrespect, discontent, and a concern for myself to the workplace.

How does this show? _____

_____

6. Am I awed by and grateful for my true Master, Jesus, and see my work as part of the dignity and privilege of serving him?

❏ Yes

❏ No

❏ Sometimes

7. Do I remember, as I work, that I will receive back from the Lord a reward that far exceeds what my employer is giving me?

❏ Yes

❏ No

❏ Sometimes

QUESTIONS FOR THOSE IN AUTHORITY

1. Does my leadership reflect the leadership of Jesus, being servant-like?

☐ Yes

☐ No

☐ Sometimes

In what way? _____

_____

2. Do I treat those under me with equal respect, care, and fairness?

☐ Yes

☐ No

☐ Sometimes

In what situations? _____

_____

3. Would I want to work for me?

☐ Yes

☐ No

☐ Maybe

Why or why not? _____

_____

4. Which is true more often?

❏ My kindness makes people want to do good work for me.

❏ My irritation, gruffness, and insecurity about my own performance make people resent working for me.

5. Which is true more often?

❏ I position myself as one who serves.

❏ I position myself as one who is powerful, important, and celebrated.

In what way? _____

_____

6. Which is true more often?

❏ I am concerned about my reputation, my success, and how I can get ahead.

❏ I try to build up the reputation, success, and advancement of those who work for me.

How does this show? _____

_____

7. Am I awed by and grateful for Jesus's servanthood toward me, wanting to be like him?

❏ Yes

❏ No

❏ Sometimes

8. Am I aware, minute-by-minute, of my Master in heaven who isn't impressed with status or position, but cares for people as people?

☐ Yes

☐ No

☐ Sometimes

When the group is ready, share some of your results. Where are you encouraged, and where do you want to grow?

How would a focus on the last two questions in each set help you with all of them?

What might change if you were more secure in the approval and love of God, and pursued it first instead of living for approval from people at work?

WRAP-UP AND PRAYER *10 MINUTES*

One good way to serve either those you work for or those who work for you is to pray for them. Spend some time praying for your workplaces and those you work with. Also pray that you would be a gospel-centered worker or boss, not just changing your behavior but doing so because you rejoice in Christ and are secure in him.

12

THE GOSPEL AND SPIRITUAL WARFARE

BIG IDEA

We most effectively engage in spiritual warfare by living in union and communion with Jesus, the divine warrior who wears the whole armor of God.

BIBLE CONVERSATION *15 MINUTES*

Paul closes his letter to the Ephesians with encouragement to stand firm. As with everything else he has written about, this too must be done "in the Lord." Have someone read **Ephesians 6:10–24** aloud. Then discuss the questions below:

In this passage, whom are the enemies a believer must stand against? How aware are you of these enemies in your day-to-day life, and why would Paul want you to be aware of them?

What is the interplay between (1) standing strong and (2) doing so "in the Lord" by using *his* power and resources? What would it look like to have the devil attack and you neglect one or the other? Give an example from your life, if you can.

According to verses 18–20, what should prayer be like for a believer who wants to be battle-ready? Which of the four uses of the word *all* in verse 18 do you most need to take to heart, and why?

****

Now take turns reading the article aloud, switching readers at the paragraph breaks. When you finish, discuss the questions that follow the article.

Lesson

ARTICLE

STRONG IN THE LORD

5 minutes

I remember the imposing plastic figure well. It was six feet tall and muscular, like a young Arnold Schwarzenegger. This stately Roman soldier was placed in front of a room full of enthusiastic elementary-age children. Welcome to Vacation Bible School, 1989.

The theme for the week was "Fighting the Battle God's Way," and I was asked to lead singing for the VBS, held in a nearby community church. Each day a new piece of armor was put on the soldier as a teaching tool for explaining Paul's warfare imagery in Ephesians 6.

The assumption was that, during his Roman imprisonment, Paul used a fully clad Roman centurion as his model for describing the equipment we must have to effectively withstand the attacks of the devil. Though many helpful insights have been drawn from this popular notion, nothing in the Bible suggests that was Paul's inspiration. It's far more likely Paul was drawing from many passages in the Old Testament, especially the book of Isaiah. There we find God himself, and the promised Messiah, wearing armor and waging war on behalf of the people of God.

This insight has given me tremendous freedom, as I'm still unlearning the less than Jesus-focused spiritual-warfare teaching

I received as a young believer. Back then, I got the impression God and Satan were engaged in a battle with an uncertain outcome. Having given us all the weaponry needed, God was up in heaven pulling for us. If we claimed the right promises, named and rebuked the right demons, kept ourselves distant from the devil's influences (and where might *that* be?), and wore the whole armor of God all the time—*then* we would enjoy the victorious Christian life. How tired, fearful, and self-preoccupied can one get?

So then, what *does* Ephesians actually teach us about spiritual warfare? And what are the implications of the gospel for how we respond to the multiple schemes of our defeated foe?

Right out of the gate, Paul puts the emphasis where it belongs. Before he says anything about the devil or spiritual warfare, he delivers a proactive admonition to all of us. "Be strong in the Lord"—that is, abide in Jesus, and let his Word abide in you. Or as Jack Miller used to say, "Live close to Jesus." Although we can't increase or decrease the unbreakable union we have with Jesus, the communion we share with him must be nourished and refreshed. As we fellowship with the Lord, we strengthen our hearts in grace.

Paul describes the God of the Bible as an armor-wearing God. He is not just the equipment manager dispensing boots, grenades, and rifles. God is the quintessential warrior himself, committed to evil's eradication and his bride's glorification. It is his armor we put on every time we "put on Christ"—a truth we will unpack later, in the exercise.

We need to know what the devil knows. The devil "knows that his time is short" (Revelation 12:12), so he is filled with fury. With his fate already determined by Jesus's cross, the devil is a master schemer. Most of his tactics seek to keep the gospel from deeply penetrating our minds and hearts. He is a tempter, seducer, accuser, and condemner—committed to paralyzing us with guilt and shame.

Satan will do anything he can to raise our suspicions about Jesus or cool our affections for him. This why Paul wrote to the Corinthians, "I feel a divine jealousy for you, since I betrothed you to one husband, to present you as a pure virgin to Christ. But I am afraid that as the serpent deceived Eve by his cunning, your thoughts will be led astray from a sincere and pure devotion to Christ" (2 Corinthians 11:2–3). The devil loves it when we are ill-religious, nominally religious, or obnoxiously religious—so long as we do not love Jesus with passion, joy, and devotion.

The devil also loves to convince us that our primary opposition in life comes from ordinary people, including members of our own household. He would rather have us cast blame on easy flesh-and-blood targets than defend ourselves against his cosmic powers and spiritual forces. Satan certainly does use people as conduits of his darkness, but the more we concentrate on knowing, worshiping, and serving Jesus, the less we'll need to worry about either blaming people or fighting demons.

Get this good news firmly established in your hearts: "The reason the Son of God appeared was to destroy the works of the devil" (1 John 3:8). Jesus appeared and he destroyed the works of the devil at the cross. "Since therefore the children share in flesh and blood, [Jesus] likewise partook of the same things, that through death he might destroy the one who has the power of death, that is, the devil" (Hebrews 2:14). Our defeated foe will be our eradicated foe one day. As Martin Luther's hymn says, "The Prince of Darkness grim, we tremble not for him. His rage we can endure, for lo, his doom is sure. One little word shall fell him." That little word will be spoken at Jesus's return.

Some days we wrestle with evil's attacks and fiery darts more than other days. Some days we actually smell the grass of the new earth breaking thought the crusty ground of our hearts and world. But *no* day requires less of Jesus than any other day. Putting on the full armor of God means looking daily at Jesus and believing his gospel.

DISCUSSION *10 MINUTES*

Think about the difference between (1) the wrong idea that Jesus is just watching you fight the devil and (2) the truth that you can take your stand because Jesus himself fights the devil. Why does the second make you more willing to resist sin? What's the difference in *how* you will resist?

In your daily life, how are you actively engaged in resisting the devil's temptations and refusing to believe his accusations? How much do you keep yourself aware, moment by moment, that Jesus has defeated him? Describe what it might look like for you to be more aware and engaged.

PUTTING ON JESUS

20 minutes

As the Messiah, Jesus fulfills the promise of every piece of armor described in Ephesians. As we live in faith union and robust communion with Jesus, this entire armament is ours.

For this exercise, read the descriptions of the armor and briefly consider what Jesus's victory in that area might mean in your life's defense against the devil. It could be:

- A certain temptation you resist
- A certain accusation the devil makes against you that you refuse to believe
- A certain fear you overcome
- A certain way to love others you undertake

Don't feel you have to come up with a specific application for every piece of armor. Just use the descriptions of Jesus as a springboard to come up with enough ideas that you have something to share when everyone is ready.

THE BELT OF TRUTH

Jesus is the belt-wearing Messiah promised by Isaiah: "Righteousness shall be the belt of his waist, and faithfulness the belt of his loins" (Isaiah 11:5). Jesus is bringing comprehensive and cosmic peace to God's broken world. He will usher in the day when the knowledge of God will fill the earth. Jesus doesn't just wear a belt of truth; he *is* the way, the truth, and the life for which we long. He is God's final word to you, "full of grace and truth" (John 1:14).

Because I know Jesus is true and brings truth, I might _____
_____.

THE BREASTPLATE OF RIGHTEOUSNESS

For the salvation of his people, Isaiah says the Lord "put on righteousness as a breastplate" (Isaiah 59:17). He did this because "all our righteous deeds are like a polluted garment" (64:6). The fulfillment of this promise happened when Jesus became your unrighteousness on the cross "so that in him we might become the righteousness of God" (2 Corinthians 5:21). Through the gospel, your whole being now wears this perfect righteousness of Christ.

Because the righteousness of Jesus covers my guilt and shame I might _____
_____.

SHOES OF READINESS AND GOSPEL PEACE

As the Messiah, Jesus came heralding the day of salvation and peace with God: "How beautiful upon the mountains are the feet of him who brings good news, who publishes peace" (Isaiah 52:7). But as Isaiah prophesied, this grand salvation grace required the substitutionary life and death of the Messiah. Jesus's feet took him to the cross so your feet can run with the gospel to the nations.

In union with Christ, you don't run from the devil. You submit yourself to Jesus and resist the devil's ploys—and it is the devil who flees from you (James 4:7).

Fitted with the shoes of gospel peace, I might be ready to _____
_____.

THE SHIELD OF FAITH

God promised Abram he would redeem a people as vast as the stars, sand, and dust. He also told Abram not to fear: "I am your shield; your reward shall be very great" (Genesis 15:1). God did not merely give a shield; God himself was the very provision and protection Abram would need to become Abraham, the father of nations. Since then, every generation of believers has joined King David in proclaiming, "The LORD is my strength and my shield; my heart trusts in him, and he helps me" (Psalm 28:7 NIV). We don't trust in faith, we trust in Jesus. Faith unites you to him, your shield.

Because Jesus is my protective shield, I might _____
_____.

THE HELMET OF SALVATION

Wearing "a helmet of salvation on his head" (Isaiah 59:17), the Lord waged a successful war against evil, sin, and death—and planted the heel of the Son squarely on the head of the serpent. You don the helmet of salvation too as you surrender your thoughts and thinking to Jesus, "in whom are hidden all the treasures of wisdom and knowledge" (Colossians 2:3).

Because I surrender my thinking to my Savior, Jesus, I might ____
_____.

THE SWORD OF THE SPIRIT

Speaking before his incarnation, the Messiah declared through Isaiah that the Lord "made my mouth like a sharp sword" (Isaiah 49:2). Jesus is the focus, the personification, and the fulfillment of the word of God, which is "living and active, sharper than any two-edged sword, piercing to the division of soul and of spirit, of joints and of marrow, and discerning the thoughts and intentions of the heart" (Hebrews 4:12). The Bible envisions the sword of the Lord coming from Jesus's mouth at his return (Revelation 19:15). He will speak eternal judgment on evil and eternal delights for you, his bride.

Because Jesus will slay my adversaries with a word, and penetrates my own heart too, I might _____
_____
_____.

Now share some of your responses with the group. What pieces of Jesus's armor do you find particularly encouraging, and why? How are you eager to resist the devil in Jesus's strength?

WRAP-UP AND PRAYER *10 MINUTES*

Paul concludes his Christ-exalting admonitions about spiritual warfare with the instruction to "pray at all times in the Spirit, with all prayer and supplication" (Ephesians 6:18). It is the Spirit's great joy to exalt Jesus in our hearts and to assure us that we are children of the Father. As we pray in the Spirit, we see Jesus enthroned at God's right hand and we cry "Abba, Father" with gratitude and confidence. And doing so, we battle well. Our faith is strengthened, and our fears topple.

Pray that beyond this study you will continue to discover the promises of God, which claim us more than we claim them. Pray in the Spirit for a life of worship and mission.

EPILOGUE: EPHESIANS 6:18-24

Paul's final words to his friends in Ephesus included a request, a gift, and a benediction. After admonishing the believers to stay alert, keep growing, and pray for each other (6:18), Paul humbles himself and asks for prayer for himself—always the mark of a great gospel leader.

Never feigning sufficiency or foolishly relying on his marvelous gifts, Paul depended on the prayers of others. He who never lacked words asked for the right words—Spirit words to boldly proclaim the gospel as an ambassador in chains in Rome, and long thereafter. He could have asked the Ephesians to pray for his release from prison, but instead his prayers were all about the advancement of the gospel.

Paul also gives the gift of encouragement, which we believers are commanded to do increasingly as the day of Jesus's return approaches (Hebrews 10:25). And Paul summarizes the heartbeat of the entire letter with a parting benediction of gospel blessings. He prays that the church will be filled with peace, love, and faith—all which find their source in God the Father and the Lord Jesus.

Jesus himself is our peace, who has destroyed hostility and reconciled us to God and to one another. All six chapters of this epistle are a testimony to God's great love for us in Jesus—the love for which we long, the only love that is "better than life" (Psalm 63:3). And faith is the gift the Father granted us to unite us to Jesus and every good thing we have in him.

Paul finishes with a flourish, adding grace to the gospel blessings he prays for the church. How fitting: he began the letter with a grace salutation, "Grace to you," and concludes with the words, "Grace be with all who love our Lord Jesus Christ with love incorruptible."

To love Jesus is, as we have seen, the primary calling of the church and each believer. We love him because he first loved us, which is quintessential grace. And only the grace of God can enable us to love Jesus with an undying, incorruptible love—for which Jesus alone is worthy.

LEADER'S NOTES

These notes provide some thoughts that relate to the study's discussion questions, especially the Bible conversation sections, from the editor who composed those questions and from the author. The discussion leader should read these notes before the study begins. Sometimes, the leader may want to refer the group to a point found here.

However, it is important that you NOT treat these notes as a way to look up the "right answer." In most cases, the best answers will be those the group discovers *on its own* through reading and thinking about the Bible passages. You will lose the value of looking closely at what the Bible says, and taking time to think about it, if you are too quick to turn to these notes.

LESSON 1: THE SO-MUCH-MORE-NESS OF THE GOSPEL

Paul's opening list of blessings we receive in Christ is both extensive and stunning: We were chosen before the foundation of the world. We were chosen to be holy and blameless before God. We were predestined to be adopted as God's children. We are works of God's will, designed to bring him praise, joined to the Savior God loves. We are redeemed (bought back) through the blood of Jesus. We are richly and graciously forgiven. We are lavished with wisdom and insight so that we understand the mysteries and purposes of God that come together in Christ. We are a part of God's grand plan for the coming age and the unity of all things. We also have an inheritance from God, the Father of all. This inheritance is so solid it was predestined for us according to God's eternal will. Its purpose could not be higher—the praise of Christ's glory. We have heard the word of truth. We have received the good news of salvation. We have been granted faith to believe. And we are sealed with the Holy Spirit so that our inheritance is guaranteed.

These are spiritual blessings "in the heavenly places." Paul wishes to set our sights on things that are unseen but are far more precious than worldly trinkets. Only with our eyes on what is heavenly will the rest of the letter make sense. The second half of the epistle, in particular, will feel like a burdensome duty unless we see the wonder of these blessings and the glory of being a participant in the eternal praise of God. Paul's list goes on and on, and then on some more—and that's the point. The beauty of the gospel and Christ's love for us is so deep we cannot see the bottom of it.

LESSON 2: GETTING THE GOSPEL DEEP INTO OUR HEARTS

Paul asks God to give *spiritual growth* to the Ephesians. In particular, he asks that the Spirit would give them godly wisdom, knowledge of God, and hearts that see what a great hope God has called them to. Paul prays that they would appreciate the riches of the gospel blessings they have: their inheritance, the power of God, and the certainty of resurrection.

For most of us, these are not things many Christians we know pray for often. But they are some of the best things we could pray for. When we know and cherish the blessings we have in Christ, they produce the gratitude, comfort, and confidence we need to live a robust Christian life. As Jesus taught, when we know our treasures are in heaven, our hearts will be there too. We will worship and come close to God—and nothing is better than him!

The fact that the gospel was already powerfully at work in the midst of the Ephesians seems to make Paul pray all the more that they would know it more deeply. Why? Because there's nothing more than the gospel, just more of the gospel! We're all just babes in the gospel. I have a good hunch we'll be in discovery mode throughout eternity.

LESSON 3: OWNING OUR NEED AND SAVORING GOD'S PROVISION

Paul tells us we are comprehensively enslaved to three tyrant rulers: the world, the devil, and our flesh. By *world* (2:2), Paul is describing how sin has invaded every sphere of God's creation, setting up a counterfeit regime, value system, and worldview. The world constantly seeks to squeeze us into its mold.

The devil—or as Paul describes him, "the prince of the air"—is the spirit who entices and empowers us for a life of rebellion and disobedience (v. 2). The apostle will have much more to say about the devil, evil, and spiritual warfare in chapter 6.

But lest we begin to think of ourselves only as victims of our world and the devil, Paul also calls out the sinful nature that beats within our own hearts. We are *willing* rebels and co-conspirators of darkness, giving into the "passions of our flesh, carrying out the desires of the body and the mind" (v. 3). We aren't merely mistake-makers, we are sin-lovers. We don't just need a new start, but a new heart.

The grace of God presented in this passage is a big-picture grace that's hugely practical in this world but also looks beyond this world: God's grace has made us alive together with Christ. It has seated us with him in the heavenly places. It exists so that God's great kindness will be displayed for all to see. It exists to put an end to boasting. It makes us able to do the good works God has prepared for us.

It should give us much wonder that God's plan of grace toward us extends to the littlest of things (small acts of goodness and humility we do each day) and also to the greatest of things (a seat in heaven and the display of God's glory). In Christ we have so much reason for joy!

LESSON 4: THE CHURCH ISN'T OPTIONAL

NOTE: Paul's statement in Ephesians 2:15 that Christ has abolished "the law of commandments expressed in ordinances" may raise questions about whether or not Christians must obey God's commands. If so, you may want to refer the group to this note. It's important to see the whole picture: God made peace with us in Jesus because it would be impossible for us to make peace with him. How did Jesus become our peace? Before he took the judgment we deserve, Jesus provided the obedience the law required. In this sense, he abolished the law of commandments. We are no longer condemned for our sin (Romans 8:1) because Jesus lived in our place and was condemned in our place (2 Corinthians 5:21). But God's moral law hasn't been *replaced* with the coming of Jesus; rather, it's been *fulfilled* for us. What's more, now Jesus also is fulfilling it *in us* by the Holy Spirit, so we do obey. But get this deep into your heart: Jesus is our substitute to trust before he is our model to follow. Only by the finished work of Jesus does the multiethnic people of God enjoy access by the Holy Spirit to our same Father, and the power and eagerness to observe God's moral law.

The passage gives us many reasons why we might be thankful to be part of God's people. *Because walls are torn down*, we live peaceably with people who are otherwise very different from ourselves. God's law no longer divides us, but joins us. We can rejoice together in the cross. We can pray together based on our joint access to our Father.

Because we are built together, we can celebrate no longer being out of place as strangers and aliens. We are citizens of heaven and members of God's family. We rest together on Jesus, the cornerstone. We are holy. We are where God dwells. We are a grace-witness that results in praise for Jesus throughout the cosmos. We are part of something *that* big and that eternally beautiful and purposeful.

The scope of this every-nation plan of redemption is breathtaking: God first announced it to Abraham in Genesis 12–17. He promised to create a great nation from Abraham, one that would exist to bless *all* families of mankind. In a sense, we could say that Israel was created to be the womb of the promised Messiah (Jesus), whose work was planned for the redemption of God's family "from every nation, from all tribes and peoples and languages" (Revelation 7:9). It is a family so big that God told Abraham to think in terms of stars, sand, and dust. Such are the mathematics of God's mercy.

Paul was humbled (and excited!) to be chosen as a narrator of God's generous unfolding plan of redemption among the Gentiles. He labels his calling "the stewardship of God's grace" (Ephesians 3:2) because, from its ancient beginning to its immeasurable end, salvation is all of grace. It's a grace-gift both to know Jesus and to serve Jesus.

To be part of Jesus's church is to have our own participation in this. The church is God's visible, live-in-the-flesh representation of his long-planned redemption. It connects us not just with each other, or with useful resources, or with a spiritual pick-me-up; it connects us with God's grand plan and with his praise throughout the cosmos.

We can speculate that if some believers in Ephesus didn't want to be part of the church, Paul might ask them how they could claim to be redeemed people but not want to be part of God's plan of redemption. Why don't they want to be part of the mystery of the ages? Why don't they want to join in the praise of the cosmos? Why don't they want to be part of proclaiming Christ to the rulers and authorities in the heavenly places? Why don't they want access in one Spirit to the Father? Why don't they want to break down walls of hostility? Why don't they want to be part of peace? Why don't they want to be a brick in God's holy temple? Why don't they want God to dwell in them?

LESSON 5: GROWING IN THE KNOWLEDGE AND LOVE OF JESUS

Paul's prayer suggests that he sees the power to live a growing Christian life first of all as being *God's power*. It is not so much our strength, but rather it comes to us because we (or in this case, Paul) have prayed to receive it from God, and because the Holy Spirit is in us as believers. It is power "through his Spirit." It is ours only because Christ dwells in us.

Secondly, this is an *inward power*, not an outward strength that will look impressive or imposing. It is something that happens "in your inner being" and "in your hearts through faith." It is "the power at work within us."

Thirdly, it is a *gospel-based power*. We gain strength to live for God as we gain comprehension of the breadth and length and height and depth of God's love toward us in Christ. And the entire strength-building process starts with "being rooted and grounded in love."

On the matter of kneeling in prayer, it is interesting to note the handful of places in the Bible where God's people adopt the relatively unusual posture of kneeling. These tend to be big and emotional moments:

- Solomon knelt at the dedication of the temple (1 Kings 8:54).
- Ezra knelt to confess Israel's sins (Ezra 9:5).

- Stephen knelt while facing martyrdom (Acts 7:60).
- Peter knelt at the death bed of Dorcas (Acts 9:40).
- Jesus knelt in Gethsemane (Luke 22:41).

CHAPTER 6: CULTIVATING A CULTURE OF GRACE

Jesus has a very specific plan for the "vibe" of his church, and it shows in how he gifts church leaders and what he appoints them to do as leaders. These leaders are supposed to (1) equip God's people for the work of ministry and (2) build them up as a body that is mature, unified, full of faith, and will eventually know Christ fully. This leadership is different from much worldly leadership in several ways.

It is *personal*. Leadership in the church is not goal-based, but people-based. Its goal is not efficiency, but maturity—to make people better and bring them closer to Jesus. This is one way Christ's leaders and his church follow the example of Christ himself, who cared about people ahead of supposed efficiency.

It is *inviting*. It brings others along and equips them to join in a grand calling, the work of Christ's kingdom. Jesus has all power and could just take over, but he gives his people the honor (and sanctifying task) of joining in his mission—even though we are very childlike when we begin.

It is *humble servitude*. Leaders in the church are not working for their own glory, but to make the people (the body of Christ) more mature and glorious. In this passage, the leaders are mentioned once and then forgotten. All the emphasis is on the rest of the church and how it grows up. This too follows Jesus's emphasis: he left his glory to take the form of a servant, making himself nothing to save his people and bring them to glory.

In this way, the church's leaders, starting with Christ himself, become a foundation of the sort of culture the church ought to possess. It is the culture described in verse 2: one of humility, gentleness, patience, and loving forbearance.

LESSON 7: REPENTANCE AND GOSPEL TRANSFORMATION

Today's passage contrasts the old self and the new self in several ways:

The old self is corrupted, not living the way human beings were created to live. The new self is created in the likeness of God, put back on track, and given power to live as God intended. The new-self life described in the second half of Ephesians is a glorious, fully human, imitating-God kind of life.

The old self is a life of deceitful desires. The new self is a life of truth and openness. There is no fakery or false pretense in the new-self life, but rather "true righteousness and holiness" (Ephesians 4:24). Several of the examples Paul gives involve truthfulness and integrity. The burden of hiding and pretending is over.

The old self is a blind life of darkness, where ignorance and callous hearts make it impossible to truly understand what is good (v. 17). The new self is a life learned directly from Christ (v. 20). We *can* have true understanding and certainty, and the ability to put off what is wrong and put on what is right and holy.

Verses 25–32 give many more insights into the new-self life through numerous examples. The description is easily recognized as a life full of compassion, gentleness, and honorable dealings with others. Even when we were unbelievers, darkened as we were, we could recognize the virtue in such a life. What a treasure that, along with forgiveness of sin, Christ works in us the gift of repentance from sin!

Gospel repentance is an inward attitude that can be boiled down to three elements: (1) an element of admission where we are aware of our sin and confess it; (2) an element of sorrow where we feel convicted and come to hate our sin; and (3) an element of turning where we redirect ourselves away from our sin and toward holy living. As we learn to become more repentant people, in the power of the Holy Spirit, we will inevitably be aware of both the old life we are forsaking and the new life we have turned toward.

NOTE ON THE EXERCISE: The exercise has the potential to discourage participants if too much attention is put on failure—the ways we still need to finish repenting of a posing and pretending life. If the leader senses this is happening, it may be helpful to remind participants that the gospel-centered life is a journey and repentance is a process. Our confidence is not based on how fully we change, but on our connection to Jesus who puts us in the process of repentance. All true believers join the process, but none arrive at its end while still in this world. The descriptions of the life of believing and repenting are not just what we "should do." They are also a joyful description of the life we aspire to and the life we will have fully one day, when we see our Savior.

LESSON 8: GOSPEL-FUELED HOLINESS

Paul presents the call to holy living as one of stark contrast to "empty words" (5:6). Holiness is a grand and most honorable calling, and at the same time one based on gratitude and love. To serve God our Father in holiness is a satisfyingly full life:

- We are imitators of God himself, a challenge so ambitious and lofty God could only give it to his most treasured and enabled creatures.
- We are beloved children, a status filled with both heavenly dignity and the precious closeness of family.

- We are people of love, a distinction of high character that describes God himself.

- We belong to the eternal Savior who gave himself up *for us*, a privilege that marks us as jewels in the crown of the King of kings and Lord of Lords—and one that might make our worship higher even that that of the angels, for we can proclaim his greatest glory personally: "Christ died *for me*."

All of this means the call to holiness is much more than a set of instructions God badgers us to follow. We pay very careful attention to it both because it consumes our deepest desires and because we realize what a travesty it would be to spurn such a calling.

To that end, here are some further notes on the teaching in this passage. The passage includes guidance on several topics that might raise questions in a group: sexual purity, greed and consumerism, and how believers should interact with the surrounding world. Especially if these questions come up, leaders may want to refer the group to the following notes:

Sin sabotages and hijacks good longings, and sexual brokenness and greed are prime examples of this. What is more basic to our identity than how we think of ourselves as sexual beings and how we steward our sexual longings toward one another? And by equating covetousness with idolatry, Paul defines greed as broken worship. The gospel is the only power great enough to reorder our affections.

Instead of assuming the right to define ourselves sexually, the gospel frees us to embrace God's design for us as sexual beings. We begin to see and grieve the ways sin has disintegrated us sexually—both as victims and participants in sexual sin. This is the beginning of the healing journey of grace.

Paul is not suggesting that anyone still dealing with sexual identity issues, sexual temptation, or sexual sin "has no inheritance in the kingdom of Christ and God"—that is, remains unconverted. If that were the case, none of us should claim to be Christians. Rather, he is saying that if we have no willingness to surrender this central aspect of our being to the teaching of Scriptures, the God of all grace, and the grace of the gospel, then our claim to be a Christian lacks credibility.

Likewise, if our over-desire—greed, lust, covetousness—for money, power, acclaim, etc., has more control over our lives than Jesus, upon what basis do we claim to be saved by his grace? Saved from what, for what? More importantly, saved for whom? These are meant to be sobering thoughts, because the issues have eternal consequences.

Holiness isn't just a personal matter, it's a corporate calling. As those redeemed by the Light of the World, Jesus says to us, "You are the light of the world. A city set on a hill cannot be hidden. Nor do people light a lamp and put it under a basket, but on a stand, and it gives light to all in the house. In the same way, let your light shine before others, so that they may see your good works and give glory to your Father who is in heaven" (Matthew 5:14–16).

The church isn't to be an ingrown group of fearful Christians, separating themselves from non-believers, exiled in "Fort God" and waiting for Jesus to return. We are to be a city set on a hill, not a club garrisoned behind closed doors. Our separation is less spatial and more spiritual. We move from partnership with darkness (Ephesians 5:7) unto partnership with Jesus who is making all things new, with our Father who is redeeming an every-nation bride, and with the Spirit who is ushering in the new creation as surely as he did with the breath of the first creation.

In union with Jesus, the church learns to "walk as children of light" (v. 8). We are to live *among* non-believers—not above them in judgment, nor behind them in embarrassment, nor under them in fear. We are to live and love among them, as good neighbors and fellow citizens. Our good lives should be much more obvious in our cities than our many views.

LESSON 9: GOSPEL-SHAPED MARRIAGE

When we look at whom the wife and husband described in this passage represent, we find that both have roles of wondrous honor in a marriage relationship—and also roles with great and godly challenges.

The wife fills the role of the church in its relationship to Jesus. We have already seen in Ephesians that the church has a breathtaking status. For example, the church is God's choice possession (1:4), his adopted children (1:5), his loved ones brought near by the blood of Christ (2:13), a reason for the praise God receives in heaven (3:10), and the Lord's light in a dark world (5:8). The church also has challenging responsibilities that fit its status and its access to God's power. For example, in submission to God the church is to lovingly bear with the failings of others (4:2), practice selfless honesty (4:25), and give thanks always and for everything (5:20). To a worldly way of thinking, taking the role of the church in submission might sound demeaning. But to people grounded in the gospel story, it is a path of staggering dignity.

The husband fills the role of Jesus in his relationship to the church. This too is a role that suggests both great honor and challenging responsibilities. Clearly, Christ is worthy of honor, but he is also the Savior who went to the cross in order to reconcile us to God (2:16), who shows us the kind of love that surpasses knowledge (3:19), and who forgives the very enemies whose sin required him to come and die (4:32). Again, to a worldly way of thinking, this put-yourself-low, sacrificing role might sound like a bad choice, or unfair. But to people grounded in the gospel story, such humility is a road to resurrection glory.

Together, a husband and wife reenact this story in little and big ways every day. What a gift it is that God has made marriage to reflect such beauty! And because its foundation is in the gospel story we *all* participate in, the deepest joys and honors of marriage are not limited to married people. Any of us who know Christ can practice submission and sacrificial love.

LESSON 10: HOME LIFE TRANSFORMED BY GRACE

The instruction for children to obey their parents comes from the fact that such obedience is "in the Lord." The core reason for obeying parents is that God has placed them in a position of authority, and we are to obey God. This means there may be situations, especially as we get older, where we see that obeying our parents is not compatible with acting "in the Lord." This should not be used as a way to avoid obedience just because we personally don't want to obey. Rather, the point is that we should have rigorous obedience toward God, which for children takes place in large part through obedience to their parents.

In much the same way, coupling the instruction to obey with the command to honor our parents increases the rigor involved and requires us to be thoughtful and deliberate in our interactions with our parents, not merely robotic. Honoring our parents takes wisdom and effort. It means controlling both our thoughts and our speech—to them and to others. And contrary to what many young people might think, it typically becomes ever harder as we and our parents age. Sometimes our parents are hardest to honor after they are dead and we are tempted to gossip about them freely!

On the parenting side, bringing up children in the Lord is far different from bringing them up in our own wisdom and the discipline we desire. It affects both what we teach them (godly truths) and how we teach them (godly, patient, faith-filled, gospel-awed practices). The article provides more detail.

LESSON 11: WORKING AS UNTO THE LORD

Masters in ancient Greco-Roman culture held more power over bondservants than most bosses in Western culture do today, so it might be natural for workers to be resentful. But Paul reminds them that their true Master is God, not any human. "Fear and trembling" may sound like a response to an abusive master, but it is also a proper response when we realize we are working for God: we take both our attitude and our work ethic very seriously. We don't just perform the outward functions of our jobs, but work from the heart. We willingly accept the position of a servant. We do not work in insecurity, chasing after the approval of others, but rather are secure in the approval of God. We do not work chiefly for worldly rewards like a paycheck, but are motivated by the heavenly rewards we will receive from our true Master.

Masters have similar responsibilities that not only guard against abuse but make the workplace a picture of the gospel and a part of Christ's realm. Harshness and threats are not the Father's way with his children, and neither should they be a Christian boss's way.

LESSON 12: THE GOSPEL AND SPIRITUAL WARFARE

Although the devil sometimes does use other people in his attacks on believers, this passage makes it clear that our real enemy is not a flesh-and-blood one. Rather, we are under attack by scheming, evil, spiritual forces. Paul is not saying this to make believers afraid, but to make us diligent. We must recognize the serious danger of our adversaries and be attentive to putting on the full armor of God, just as a soldier would be careful not to be without any part of his armor if he knew dangerous enemies were attacking.

It would be foolhardy and extremely dangerous for a soldier to face the enemy without his armor. In the same way, no believer should try—or be urged—to face the devil's temptations and accusations in his own strength and determination. The pieces of armor mentioned all speak of Jesus and the blessings we have in him. These are our strength and protection when the devil comes against us, and we cannot stand if we neglect to hold them close. Of course, it would be equally wrong to possess all the armor (to know the gospel backward and forward) but then neglect to stand and fight in that armor. The Christian life is always a matter of diligently resisting the temptations and accusations of the evil one, but also always doing so in the strength and assurances our God alone provides. We fight *with* our Savior, not as a performance *for* him.

By placing his discussion of prayer at the end of the armor imagery, Paul suggests that prayer is a key way we acquire this armor and engage the fight alongside our God who is already in battle. For a Christian warrior, prayer is no tack-on item at the end of the real agenda. We are to pray at *all* times, for *all* needs, with *all* perseverance, for *all* the saints. Most of us need to take every one of these *all* instructions to heart. They are how we resist evil (and, indeed, how we live the entire Christian life) "in the Lord and in the strength of his might."

A GOSPEL GLOSSARY

JUSTIFICATION

As soon as we put our faith in Jesus, God forgave all our sins (past, present, and future—all sins of thought, word, and deed). He also declared us to be legally righteous in his sight. He credited to us the righteousness of Jesus. God put every good, godly, loving thing Jesus did during his life into our account, as though we did those things.

Justification highlights the fact that Jesus didn't primarily come into the world to be our model to follow (so that we might earn salvation), but to be our substitute to trust (that we might receive salvation as a gift). He fulfilled the law for us by his life of perfect obedience. Jesus is the second Adam, not our second chance.

God imputed Christ's righteousness to us, securing us in the legal status of a perfectly righteous person. Therefore, God cannot possibly love us more than he does right now, and he will never love us less. In fact, he loves us just as much as he loves Jesus, and there's nothing we can do to alter it. We cannot add to this standing in grace nor diminish it.

Justification deals with longings and questions like:

- What am I to do with my guilt and sense of not measuring up?
- Will I ever be good enough, in God's eyes or my own?
- Does God love me more when I'm obedient and less when I screw up?
- How can I get free from living for people's approval?

PROPITIATION

Much as Jesus's righteousness has been legally declared ours, so all of our sins have been legally declared to belong to Jesus. They were imputed (credited) to Jesus on the cross. He died in our place, the righteous for the unrighteous. Jesus was treated as though he did all the unloving, ungodly, unjust things we have done. Jesus gladly went to the cross for us—so great is his love and sacrifice for us.

This means that when Jesus died on the cross, God exhausted his judgment against us and our sins. The cross was our judgment day. We don't have to be afraid of dying and facing judgment. God will never deal with us according to our sins again because he dealt with Jesus according to our sins. God will discipline us in love as a Father, but he will never punish us as a judge.

Propitiation deals with longings and questions like:

- How can I be free from my shame?
- What will happen when I die and have to face God's judgment?
- How can I be certain God won't pay me back for all the bad stuff I've done?
- What really happened on the cross when Jesus died?

ADOPTION

As soon as we put our trust in Jesus, we were legally adopted into God's family. Instantaneously, we were given all the rights and delights of a beloved child of God. We can never lose this status and standing. God even placed his Holy Spirit in our hearts to seal us as his child and to constantly whisper (sometimes shout!) that we are no longer orphans or slaves, but his passionately loved and treasured children. We cannot intensify nor diminish God's fatherly affection for us.

Adoption deals with longings and questions like:

- What does God think about me all day long?
- What am I to do with my longings for intimacy, advocacy, and care?
- Is there any hope that I can become a relationally healthy person?
- What am I to do when my marriage, kids, and friends aren't enough?

SANCTIFICATION

Sanctification is the lifelong process of becoming more and more like Jesus. Like our justification, sanctification is entirely a work of grace—a gift to us—which is why growing up in Jesus is called growth in grace. There is no room for earning or meriting anything in our sanctification. God doesn't love us to the degree we are like Jesus, but to the degree we are in Jesus—which is 100 percent!

Yet, this end to all earning is not an end to all effort. One sign that we are being sanctified is that when we see more of Jesus's beauty and righteousness, it also causes us to see more of our sin and brokenness, and this drives us to surrender to the work of the Spirit in our lives. We devote ourselves to the means of grace—the things God uses to grow us up.

This includes Bible study, prayer, fellowship, corporate worship, etc. Growing in grace means not just growing as characters in God's great story of redemption but also growing as carriers of that story. Every believer is called to a life of purposeful, missional engagement as we seek to make disciples of all nations. Reaching out to others is one of the primary ways we see more clearly just how deep our need for Jesus truly is. Again, these things don't earn us anything or put a bigger smile on God's face. But they are profitable to us and are conduits of God's grace.

As we grow, God will show us what is repent-able and what is repairable in our lives. We are all both agents and victims of sin, and we need both change and healing. This journey will continue throughout our lives and will only be completed when we die or Jesus returns.

Sanctification deals with longings and questions like:

- What hope do I have that I can actually change?
- What does the process of change look and feel like?
- I know Jesus has forgiven me, but what am I to do with my pain?
- How come it's taking me so long to get better?

GLORIFICATION

Glorification is the magnificent completion of our salvation, which God promised and will provide at Jesus's return. One day, we will be as lovely and loving as Jesus. We cannot become "un-born again." We will never have our citizenship in heaven revoked. We are destined to live as a beautiful us, with our beautiful God, in a beautiful world (the new heavens and new earth, the fully restored and renewed universe). All of our relationships will be perfect, our bodies will be resurrected and will never wear out, and all death and mourning and evil and brokenness will be gone forever.

Glorification deals with longings and questions like:

- Can I risk having hope for myself, others, and the world I live in?

- What is this world coming to? It feels so scary, out-of-control, and evil.

- What is heaven really going to be like?

- Can I really trust God to heal, restore, free, and make me whole?

- How do I know I won't lose my salvation or be kicked out of God's family?